Southern Elegance

A SECOND COURSE

D1399550

JUNIOR LEAGUE OF GASTON COUNTY, NORTH CAROLINA

Published by
Junior League of Gaston County, N.C.

Copyright © 1999
Junior League of Gaston County, N.C.
2950 South Union, Suite A
Gastonia, North Carolina 28054

Library of Congress Catalog Number: 98-075109
ISBN: 0-9621734-1-X
Suggested Retail: $17.95

Designed and Manufactured by
Favorite Recipes® Press
an imprint of

FRP™

P.O. Box 305142
Nashville, Tennessee 37230
800-358-0560
Manufactured in the United States of America

*The Junior League of Gaston County, North Carolina, Inc.
will strive to build strong financial and volunteer support for
the health and well being of women and children through
program development and community partnerships.
Cookbook Committee*

Introduction

Miles of sandy beaches with gently rolling waves, mountain foliage on fire with a burst of autumn color, front porches with ferns swaying gently in the summer breeze, and the explosion of new life seen in the blossoms of magnolias, azaleas, and dogwoods. These are just a few of the images that come to mind when you think of the South.

There is something more than these splendid images, which draws people to our Piedmont area. It is our gracious way of living and Southern hospitality.

Food is such a vital part of our way of life. It is the center of all our celebrations and gatherings from births, baptisms, birthdays, graduations, weddings, sporting events, and holidays to funerals. It does more than nourish our bodies. It is a loving extension of ourselves nourishing the minds, hearts, and spirits of those we love, as well. Recipes, both those handed down from generation to generation and new ones are a link to our pasts and a bridge to our future.

The collection of recipes found within are treasures reflecting the blessings of the seasons and the heritage and traditions of the families represented.

Southern Elegance, A Second Course, offers wonderful new recipes and menus in the same gracious style as our first cookbook, Southern Elegance. One of our most exciting sections, Holiday and Gift Giving, celebrates the spirit of Southern generosity. The recipes and gift ideas in this section represent handmade gifts for the young and young at heart.

The pineapple, a symbol characteristic of Southern hospitality, is found throughout our book. Wherever it is found, there is a helpful hint to enrich your cooking and entertaining.

As the Junior League of Gaston County embarks on our fortieth year, we pay tribute to our past presidents in a special section, Southern Inspirations. This section contains recipes, which are and have been special to them. We thank them for all they have done to nourish and inspire our lives and the lives of those in Gaston County, and we look forward to nourishing and inspiring the lives of generations to come.

Committee/Acknowledgements

Lindsay Lockett, *Chairman*
Janet Long, *Co-Chairman*
Susan R. Schultz, *Co-Chairman*

Sherry Abernethy   Robin Hackney
Amy Boyd   Julie Heath
Beth Brittain   Ginger Hinman
Shelly Carter   Patti Hunter
Josie Conner   Terri Nixon
Audrey Devine   Denise Smith
Diane Driscoll   Leslie Wallace

*Cover Art by the late Scott Barnes, reproduced with her family's permission.
This is the second Scott Barnes' print that has been used by the Junior League
of Gaston County for use in* Southern Elegance *cookbooks, and it is with
deep appreciation that we acknowledge this family's commitment
to the League's goals and objectives.*

Holt Harris, Artist
*Holt has blessed us yet again with her talent to add life to our cookbook
through her artwork. We sincerely appreciate her dedication and generosity.*

*We thank all of the Junior League members who shared recipes with us.
A special thanks to Karen Minton for beginning our project. We also thank
Cindy Kase and Laura Newman for their help with typesetting.*

Contents

Southern Occasions

Appetizers Before the Heart Ball

Bloody Marys

Barbequed Shrimp

Artichoke and Bleu Cheese Dip

Boursin and Assorted Crackers

Panthers Tailgate Party

Tarheel Tailgate Special

Flank Steak Sandwiches

Orzo Pasta Salad

Baked Corn in the Husk

Sundrop Cake or Coca-Cola Cake

ACC Championship Party
It's a Guy Thing

Coyote Caviar with Tortilla Chips

Soup for the Slopes

Broccoli Corn Bread

White Chocolate Chunk Cookies

Beer and Soft Drinks

Committee Meeting at Your House

Green Punch

Shrimp Dip

German Chocolate Cream Cheese Bars

Chocolate Covered Pretzel Mix

Dustpan Snack Mix

Grown-Up Mother-Daughter Tea Party

Victoria Sandwich Cake

Mixed Fresh Fruit with Heavenly Dressing

Ham and Broccoli Quiche Tarts

Special Almond Iced Tea

Assorted Hot Teas

Gourmet Supper Club

Sun-Dried Tomato Pesto on Baked Brie

Pecan and Cheese Crumble Salad

Lime Tarragon Grilled Salmon

Island Yams

Applesauce Cheese Biscuits

Decadent Chocolate Chip Cheesecake

Kahlúa and Coffee or Hazelnut Café au Lait

Christmas Eve Open House

Maggie's Cheese Ball and Patsy's Crab Cake Appetizers

Stuffed Snow Peas

Tomato Aspic and Cream Cheese Salad

Fruit Casserole

Janet's Favorite Marinade with London Broil

served with Assorted Rolls

Triple Layer Chocolate Cheesecake and Pumpkin Cheesecake Bars

Family Birthday Party

Cheesy Chicken Breasts

Hash Brown Potatoes

Impossible Zucchini Tomato Pie

Easy Biscuits

Chocolate Fudge Birthday Cake

"Sip & See" for Wedding Gifts or New Baby

Raspberry Punch

Petit Tomato Pies

Greek Wedding Cookies

Susan's Breakfast Bites

Deviled Eggs with Sun-Dried Tomatoes and Chives

Strawberry Bread

Spring Brunch

Champagne Punch

Breakfast Shrimp and Grits

Raspberry Green Beans or Asparagus Casserole

Old Fashioned Stickies

Mango Parfaits

Appetizers

Cheddar-Apple Dip

8 ounces cream cheese, softened
1/4 cup mayonnaise
1/2 cup cheddar cheese, shredded
1/2 cup apples, finely chopped

Combine cream cheese and
mayonnaise, blending well. Stir in
cheddar cheese and apples. Serve
with crackers and apple wedges.
May use reduced-fat cream cheese,
cheddar cheese and mayonnaise.

—Betsy Forbes

Sun-Dried Tomato Pesto on Baked Brie

Prepare ahead
Serves 4–6

1/4 cup sun-dried tomatoes, chopped
    (not oil packed)
2 teaspoons olive oil
2 garlic cloves, minced
2 teaspoons balsamic vinegar
1/2 teaspoon dried basil
1/4 cup fresh parsley, chopped
fresh, ground pepper to taste
1 medium or 2 small rounds Brie cheese

Cover chopped, sun-dried tomatoes
with boiling water. Let stand 15
minutes. Drain. In a small skillet,
heat oil over medium low heat. Cook
tomatoes, garlic, vinegar and basil
for 1 minute. Remove from heat. Stir
in parsley and pepper. Let cool. Cut
rind off top of cheese. Place cheese on
baking sheet and top with tomato
mixture. Bake in a 350 degree oven
for 5 to 10 minutes or until cheese
melts slightly. Serve with crackers.

—Barbara Emerson

Roquefort Cheesecake

Prepare ahead
Serves 16

1 1/2 tablespoons butter
1/2 cup bread crumbs
1/4 cup Parmesan cheese
1/2 pound bacon
1 medium onion, chopped
1 3/4 pounds cream cheese, softened
1/2 pound Roquefort or bleu cheese
4 eggs
1/3 cup cream
1/2 teaspoon salt
few drops hot sauce

Butter a 9 or 10 inch springform
pan and sprinkle with bread crumbs
and Parmesan. Fry bacon and
crumble. Cook onion in 1 tablespoon
bacon grease. Cream together cream
cheese and Roquefort cheese. Add
eggs, cream and seasonings. Blend
until smooth. Fold in bacon and
onion. Pour into prepared pan and
set in large pan of hot water. Bake
at 325 degrees for 1 hour and 20
minutes. Cut oven off and cool
in oven for 1 hour. Cool to room
temperature before removing
from pan. Serve with crackers or
fruit slices.   —Anne D. Decker

Hot Cheese Dip

Prepare ahead
Serves a crowd

16 ounces cream cheese (may use fat
    free), softened
1 small onion, chopped
1 pound sharp cheddar cheese, grated
1 jar of chipped beef, shredded
1/4 to 1/2 can chilies
1/2 teaspoon garlic powder
4 dashes Worcestershire sauce
1 bell pepper, chopped
1 loaf round bread, hollowed out

Combine all ingredients and put
into loaf of bread. Bake 20 minutes
at 350 degrees or until heated all
the way through. Goes well with
wheat crackers.

          —Theresa F. McIntosh

Cheesy Jalapeño Squares

Prepare ahead
Serves 12

1 (4-ounce) can jalapeños, chopped or
    green chilies, chopped
6 eggs, beaten well
1 pound sharp cheddar cheese, grated

Grease a 2-quart baking dish and
spread a layer of the chopped
jalapeños. Sprinkle cheese over the
peppers. Pour beaten eggs evenly
over the cheese. Bake at 350 degrees
for 1 hour. Cool and cut into squares.
          —Robin Pauli

Cheese Pastries

Prepare ahead
Yield 3 dozen

1/2 cup butter, softened
1 cup sharp cheddar cheese, shredded
1 cup all-purpose flour
1/8 teaspoon cayenne pepper
pinch salt
2 tablespoons cold water
3 dozen pitted dates
3 dozen pecan halves

Preheat oven to 400 degrees. Cream
butter and cheese in medium bowl
until smooth. Combine flour,
cayenne pepper and salt in small
bowl. Add to cheese mixture along
with water and stir until all dry
ingredients are moistened. Roll
dough to 1/8-inch thickness on
lightly floured surface and cut into
2-inch squares. Cut a slit in each
date and fill with pecan half. Place
the filled date in the center of each
pastry overlapping slightly and
press gently to seal. Place pastry on
greased sheet and bake 15 minutes
or until lightly browned.
          —Renee Steelman Long

*As a rule, count on one-quarter
cup of dip per person as an appetizer.*

Artichoke and Bleu Cheese Dip

Prepare ahead
Serves 12

1 stick of butter
1 (14-ounce) can of artichoke hearts
1 (4-ounce) package bleu cheese
lemon juice to taste

In a skillet, melt butter and mix in artichoke hearts. Cut in eighths. Add bleu cheese and lemon juice. Serve in hot chafing dish with rye cracker rounds.

—Vanessa M. Stewart

Braunschweiger Spread

Prepare ahead
Serves a crowd

1/2 pound braunschweiger
3 to 4 ounces cream cheese, softened
1 tablespoon horseradish
dash of Worcestershire sauce
steak sauce or compatible seasoning

Mix braunschweiger with cream cheese. Add horseradish, dash of Worcestershire and steak sauce to taste. Refrigerate at least 1 hour before serving. Spread on crackers or sandwiches.   —Amy S. McHenry

Bruschetta

Serve immediately
Serves 12

1 loaf French bread
crushed garlic
olive oil
6 Roma tomatoes (sizes may vary the number needed)
chèvre cheese
1 (4-ounce package) feta cheese
fresh or dried basil
oregano
Parmesan cheese (optional)

Preheat oven to 350 degrees. Thinly slice bread. Toast in 350 degree oven for 10 minutes. Spread with a little garlic. Drizzle with olive oil. Thinly slice tomatoes and put a slice or two on each slice of bread. Crumble some of both cheeses over bread slices. Sprinkle each slice with basil, oregano, salt and pepper to taste (and Parmesan if you like.) Bake at 400 degrees for 5 minutes. Enjoy. Note: any cheeses may be used.

—Denise Smith

Spinach Balls

Freeze before cooking
Serves 10

2 (10-ounce) packages frozen chopped
   spinach
2 cups packaged herb stuffing
3/4 cup butter, melted
1/2 teaspoon thyme
dash pepper
6 eggs, beaten
1/4 cup onion, finely chopped
1 large garlic clove, minced
1 cup Parmesan cheese, grated

Cook spinach according to directions
on package. Drain well. Mix together
spinach, stuffing, butter, thyme,
pepper, eggs, onion, garlic and
Parmesan cheese. Form into balls.
Place on cookie sheet and freeze.
Bake frozen spinach balls for 20
minutes at 350 degrees.

—Lori Rutherford

Baked Spinach Dip

Quick to prepare
Serves a crowd

1 (10-ounce) package of frozen spinach
1 (12-ounce) jar marinated artichoke
   hearts
3 garlic cloves, minced
1/2 cup mayonnaise
1 (12-ounce) package cream cheese,
   softened
2 tablespoons lemon juice
1 cup Parmesan cheese, grated
1 cup bread crumbs

Preheat oven to 375 degrees. Drain
spinach and artichoke hearts. Mix
all ingredients together and put in
a greased baking dish. Sprinkle
bread crumbs over top and bake 30
minutes. Serve warm with crackers or
bread. Delicious!

—Vicky West Heinrich

*To facilitate flattening bread slices for rolled party sandwiches, steam slices of
bread in a colander over boiling water for a minute or two. The bread will
then roll easily.*

Stuffed Mushrooms

Serve immediately
Serves 6–8

1 large carton of large fresh mushrooms,
   rinsed, dried and stems cut out
8 ounces cream cheese, softened
1 cup Parmesan cheese
dash salt
dash nutmeg
2 dashes Worcestershire sauce
dash hot sauce

Mix cream cheese, Parmesan cheese,
salt, nutmeg, Worcestershire sauce
and hot sauce together. Stuff
mushrooms with the above mixture.
Roll in Parmesan cheese and bake
15 minutes at 350 degrees on a
greased baking pan. Mushrooms
need to be served hot.   —Pam Paige

"It's a Guy Thing"

Prepare ahead
Freezes well
Serves 15–20

"Men love this recipe."

1 pound ground beef
1 pound sausage
1 pound Velveeta chesse
1 teaspoon oregano
1/2 teaspoon garlic salt
1 loaf party rye bread

Brown ground beef and sausage
together; drain. Cube the cheese and
melt into the meat mixture. Add
seasonings. Simmer 1 to 2 minutes.
Place 1 tablespoon onto each slice
of party rye; place on baking sheet.
Bake at 375 degrees 8 to 10 minutes
or until bubbly.   —Beth Harwell

*Store toothpicks in an empty spice bottle with a shaker top and screw-on lid. It is
easy to remove the lid and gently shake out a toothpick through the holes when you
need one. They will always be clean and handy.*

Boursin

Prepare ahead
Serves 8–12

"Excellent for dinner club or get-togethers"

2 (8-ounce) packages cream cheese,
 softened
2 garlic cloves, crushed
2 teaspoons basil
2 teaspoons chives
2 teaspoons dill weed
lemon-pepper seasoning

Mix all ingredients except lemon-pepper and shape into a ball. Roll in lemon-pepper seasoning; refrigerate. Serve with bland crackers.

—Susan R. Schultz

Crab Dip

Serve immediately
Serves 12

1 pound crab meat, canned is fine to use
 or may use imitation
1 cup mild cheddar cheese, shredded
1 cup sour cream
3 ounces cream cheese, softened
1 teaspoon mustard
3 teaspoons Worcestershire sauce

Thoroughly mix sour cream, cream cheese, mustard, and Worcestershire. Fold in crab meat and cheddar cheese. Bake at 350 degrees for 30 minutes. Serve with crackers!

—Lisa M. Rouse

Shrimp Dip

Prepare ahead
Serves 50

4 (8-ounce) packages cream cheese,
 softened
3 medium onions, grated
dash of Worcestershire sauce
1 cup cocktail sauce
2 pounds boiled shrimp, cut into pieces

Cream the softened cheese. Add onions, Worcestershire and cocktail sauce and mix well. Fold in the shrimp pieces.　　—Cathy Barrett

Pickled Shrimp

Prepare 1 day ahead
Serves 4–6

1 1/2 or 2 pounds shrimp, cooked
1 cup Wesson oil
1/2 cup vinegar
3 shakes hot pepper sauce
2 tablespoons Worcestershire sauce
2 teaspoons salt
pepper to taste
1 tablespoon dried mustard
1/2 teaspoon paprika
1 onion, sliced
2 bay leaves

Combine all ingredients and
refrigerate for 24 hours prior
to serving.   —Angie Huggins

Cheese Ball

Prepare ahead
Yields 1 ball

8 ounces cream cheese, softened
8 ounces Velveeta sharp cheese
1 (8-ounce) box chopped dates
1 cup pecans, crushed

Mix cheeses well, pour in dates and
kneed with hands. Roll into a ball
and add nuts to cover outside. Keep
refrigerated until ready to serve
with crackers.   —Leslie Wallace

Black Bean Salsa

Must prepare ahead
Serves 12–15

"May be used as an appetizer with
tortilla chips, as a sauce over grilled
seafood, or as a salad."

1 (15-ounce) can black beans, drained
    and rinsed
1 (11-ounce) can white shoepeg corn,
    drained
2 medium tomatoes, diced
1 red bell pepper, chopped
1 green bell pepper, chopped
1/2 cup red onion, diced
2 to 3 fresh jalapeño peppers, sliced thin
1/3 cup fresh cilantro, finely chopped

Marinade:
1/3 cup fresh lime juice
1/3 cup olive oil
1 teaspoon salt
1/2 teaspoon cumin
1/2 teaspoon cayenne pepper

Combine all ingredients except for
marinade ingredients. Combine
marinade ingredients in a jar. Stir or
shake until mixed. Pour over other
ingredients to mix. Let marinate
several hours in the refrigerator.
          —Janice W. Stowe

Caponata

Prepare ahead
Yields 4 cups

"While time-consuming to make, it is well worth the effort. It is delicious when using fresh ingredients from a well stocked summer garden!"

2 cups eggplant, cubed and peeled
1 teaspoon coarse sea salt
4 tablespoons olive oil
1 cup onion, chopped
1/2 cup green bell pepper, chopped
1/2 cup red bell pepper, chopped
3/4 cup celery, chopped
2 cups tomatoes, crushed
1/2 teaspoon coarse black pepper
1/2 teaspoon dried oregano
1/2 teaspoon dried basil
1 tablespoon garlic, minced
1 tablespoon Italian parsley, chopped
1/2 cup calamata olives, chopped
2 tablespoons capers, drained

Place the eggplant in a colander, sprinkle it with coarse salt and let it drain for 1 hour. Heat 2 tablespoons of the oil in a large flameproof casserole or Dutch oven. Pat the eggplant dry with paper towels, and add it to the casserole. Sauté over medium heat until soft and lightly browned, about 10 minutes. Using a slotted spoon, remove the eggplant and set it aside. Add the remaining oil, then the onion, bell peppers and celery to the casserole. Sauté over medium heat until the vegetables are softened, about 10 minutes. Return the eggplant to the casserole. Add the tomatoes, pepper, oregano, basil, garlic, parsley, olives, and capers. Simmer until the vegetables are tender, about 45 minutes. Serve hot or at room temperature in "one-bite" bread cups or as a spread on pita points or crackers.   —Shelly Carter

Easy Cheesy Dip

Serves 8

1 cup onion, chopped
1 cup cheddar cheese, shredded
1 cup mayonnaise
1 cup sour cream

Mix all ingredients together. Bake at 350 degrees in serving dish until bubbly. Serve with crackers.

—Amy Boyd

To mold individual appetizers, use miniature muffin tins or styrofoam egg cartons.

Deep Dish Pizza Dip

Serve immediately
Serves 6–8

"Great sporting or party appetizer"

8 ounces cream cheese, softened
$1/2$ cup sour cream
1 teaspoon oregano
1 teaspoon garlic, minced
1 teaspoon red pepper
1 (15-ounce) jar pizza sauce
1 small onion, diced
2 cups mozzarella cheese, shredded
1 box wheat crackers
pepperoni to taste

Beat together cream cheese and
sour cream. Spread in the bottom
of 1 quart Pyrex dish. Spread onion
over top. Sprinkle oregano, garlic and
red pepper on top of onions. Spread
pizza sauce over top. Slice pepperoni
and spread on top to taste. Bake
at 375 degrees for 15 minutes.
Remove from oven and add 2 cups
of mozzarella cheese. Broil until
cheese melts. Serve with wheat
crackers to dip. —Tifany Gray

Coyote Caviar Served with Tortilla Chips

Prepare ahead

1 (15-ounce) can black beans, rinsed
   and drained
1 (4-ounce) can chopped ripe olives,
   rinsed and drained
1 small onion, finely chopped
1 (4-ounce) can diced green chilies
1 garlic clove, finely chopped
4 tablespoons fresh cilantro, chopped
2 tablespoons vegetable oil
2 tablespoons fresh lime juice
2 teaspoons chili powder
$1/4$ teaspoon salt
$1/4$ teaspoon crushed red pepper
$1/4$ teaspoon cumin
1 teaspoon pepper
8 ounces cream cheese, softened
2 hard cooked eggs, peeled and chopped
green onions, chopped

Mix all ingredients except cream
cheese, eggs, and green onion. Cover
this bean mixture and chill at least
2 hours or overnight. Spread softened
cream cheese on a round serving
plate. Spoon bean mixture evenly
over cream cheese. Arrange chopped
eggs around the edge of the bean
mixture. Sprinkle the green onions
on top. —Patti Hunter

Beverages & Breads

Hazelnut Café au Lait

Serve hot
Serves 3

3 cups skim or 1% milk
2 tablespoons chocolate-hazelnut spread
2 cups brewed coffee
ground cinnamon for garnish

Heat milk and hazelnut spread in a microwave oven or saucepan, stirring frequently, until the mixture starts to steam. Do not boil. Blend in coffee and divide among three serving cups, dusting with cinnamon.   —Betse Huston

Yellow Birds

Serve chilled
Serves 8–10

8 ounces creme de banana liqueur
8 ounces light rum
4 ounces unsweetened pineapple juice
2 ounces lemon juice
4 ounces orange juice

Combine all ingredients in a large pitcher. Chill. Serve over crushed ice in pretty punch or julep cups.
                 —Renee Long

Dad's Whiskey Sour

Freezes well
May prepare ahead
Serves 6–8

"A Tarheel Tailgate Special"

1 (6-ounce) can frozen lemonade
*   concentrate*
2 cans bourbon
3 cans water

Mix lemonade, bourbon and water. Freeze overnight. This will be frozen slush the next day. Pour in a blender and mix. Then put into cooler jugs for travel purposes to football games. If serving these right after mixing, use one 6 ounce can of lemonade concentrate and 1 can of bourbon. Mix in blender with chipped ice and no water. Pour into glasses.
                 —Mrs. William N. Thrower, Jr.

Coffee kept in the refrigerator will stay fresh longer.

McKibbin Punch

May prepare ahead
Serves 16–20

3 quarts pineapple juice
1 1/2 cups lemon juice
3 cups orange juice
1/3 cup lime juice
2 (1-quart) bottles carbonated water
2 1/2 cups sugar
4 (1-quart) bottles ginger ale
frozen strawberries
sliced lemons and limes

Combine juices and sugar and chill. Fill a bundt pan 1/4 full with mixture. Add strawberries, lemons, and limes to pan and freeze. Add additional fruit and juice and freeze. Continue freezing juice and fruit in layers until bundt pan is full. Place chilled juices in a large punch bowl. Add ginger ale and carbonated water and stir. Add frozen ring and serve.

—Laura Calhoun Dixon

Nanny's Banana Punch

May prepare ahead
Serves 20 or more

"My mother-in-law has made this for years and it is a summer favorite of family and friends!"

2 cups sugar
3 cups water
1/4 cup lemon juice
1 1/2 cups orange juice
3 bananas, crushed well
46 ounces pineapple juice
2 quarts ginger ale

Dissolve sugar in water. Mix with lemon juice, orange juice, bananas, and pineapple juice. Freeze. Take out of freezer and let sit awhile before putting in punch bowl. It will come out of the container more easily. Put frozen mixture in punch bowl and add ginger ale.   —Josie Conner

Percolator Punch

Serve warm
Serves 20

"Serve warm on a cold winter night."

1 (48-ounce) can pineapple juice
1 (48-ounce) can cranberry apple juice
24 ounces water
2 tablespoons brown sugar
ground cinnamon
3 sticks whole cinnamon
several whole cloves
dash of salt

Put juice and water in the bottom of a large percolator. In the top, place the rest of the ingredients. Plug in percolator and heat until warm.

—Shelby Rhyne

Make homemade wine coolers with 1/2 part wine, 1/4 part orange juice, and 1/4 part lemon-lime carbonated drink.

Easy Sangria

May serve over ice
Serves approximately 24

2 (12-ounce) cans frozen pink lemonade, thawed, undiluted
1 (33-ounce) bottle Rosé, chilled
1 (33-ounce) bottle Burgundy, chilled
juice of 2 limes, more if you prefer
1 (32-ounce) bottle club soda, chilled
1/2 lime, lemon and orange, thinly sliced

Combine lemonade, Rosé, Burgundy, and lime juice. Mix well. Add club soda slowly. Garnish with lime, lemon and orange slices.

—Mrs. John B. Garrett, Jr.

Mr. Allen's Old Crow Punch

Quick to prepare
Serves 20

"I obtained this recipe from my husband's aunt, Julie Hoell, who lives in Washington, N.C."

1 fifth Old Crow
1 (6-ounce) can frozen lemonade, partially thawed
1 (6-ounce) can frozen orange juice, partially thawed
1/3 cup cherry juice
1 quart club soda

Mix all ingredients together. Serve in a punch bowl and garnish with clove-studded oranges. May float ice ring in punch bowl, if desired.

—Kristie Smith

Cheery Cherry Lemonade

Serves 20 preschoolers

"This is a favorite at Presbyterian Weekday School in Gastonia, N.C.!"

juice of 6 lemons
1 (2-liter) bottle ginger ale
1 quart ice water
2 cups sugar
1 (10-ounce) jar red cherries,
   including juice

Combine lemon juice with sugar and ice water. Stir to dissolve sugar. Stir in cherries and cherry juice. Add ginger ale and serve.

—Ginger Hinman

Church Picnic Lemonade

Serve chilled
Yields 1 gallon

juice of 3 lemons
2 packets unsweetened lemonade mix
2¹/₂ to 3 cups sugar
water to fill a 1-gallon container
additional lemon, sliced for garnish

Combine lemon juice, lemonade, sugar and water. Stir to dissolve sugar. Serve well chilled with lemon slices to garnish. —Ginger Hinman

Apricot Punch

Chill before serving
May prepare ahead
Freezes well
Serves 10–12

1 (3-ounce) box of apricot jello
2 cups sugar
2 cups hot water
4 tablespoons fresh lemon juice
46 ounces canned pineapple juice
1 quart of water (can add another
   quart of water to suit taste)

Mix jello, sugar and hot water. Stir until dissolved. Add the remaining ingredients. Chill and serve.

—Susan Allen

For additional beverages, please see the Breakfast/Brunch section.

Delicious Pumpkin Bread

Freezes well
Makes 4 (1-pound) loaves

"This bread makes a great
Christmas gift!"

4 cups sugar
1 (29-ounce) can pumpkin
3 eggs
1 cup vegetable oil
5 cups all-purpose flour
1 tablespoon baking soda
2 teaspoons cinnamon
1 1/2 teaspoons ground cloves
1 teaspoon salt
2 cups coarsely chopped dates
2 cups coarsely chopped toasted walnuts
whipped cream cheese (optional)

Preheat oven to 350 degrees. Grease
four 1-pound coffee cans or 4x8-inch
pans. Combine sugar, pumpkin and
eggs in large bowl and beat by hand
or with mixer until well-blended.
Add oil and beat to combine.
Thoroughly blend in flour, soda,
cinnamon, cloves and salt. Stir in
dates and nuts. Fill prepared pans
3/4 full to allow for rising during
baking. Bake 1 hour or until toothpick inserted near center of loaf
comes out clean and bread has pulled
away slightly from sides of pan. Serve
with whipped cream cheese. Breads
may be frozen indefinitely.

   —Mary Loughridge Sessoms

Favorite Pumpkin Muffins

1 stick margarine, softened
1 1/2 cups sugar
2 large, overripe bananas
1/2 can pumpkin
2 eggs
1/2 teaspoon vanilla extract
2 cups all-purpose flour
1 teaspoon baking soda
1/4 teaspoon salt
1 1/2 teaspoons cinnamon
1/4 teaspoon nutmeg
1/4 teaspoon cloves
1/2 teaspoon ginger

Cream together sugar and margarine.
Mash bananas, add pumpkin and
eggs; mix with margarine and sugar.
Stir in vanilla. Sift together dry
ingredients and mix with pumpkin
mixture. (May add raisins or nuts if
you please.) Pour into greased pans—
makes 1 large loaf or 4 small loaves
or a big batch of muffins. Bake at
350 degrees for about 45 minutes
for a large loaf, 25 to 40 minutes for
small loaves or muffins. I usually
double this recipe to use a whole can
of pumpkin.   —Ginger Hinman

Sour Cream Banana Bread

Prepare ahead
Freezes well

3 tablespoons margarine, softened
1 cup sugar
1 egg
1/2 cup sour cream
2 cups all-purpose flour
1/2 teaspoon salt
2 teaspoons baking powder
1 teaspoon baking soda
3/4 cup mashed bananas
1 tablespoon lemon juice

Cream butter and sugar until light and fluffy. Add egg and sour cream. Combine dry ingredients; alternately add to creamed mixture along with bananas, mixing well after each addition. Add lemon juice, stirring until blended. Spoon into greased and floured loaf pan. Bake at 375 degrees for 50 minutes.

—Christy Luce

Strawberry Bread

May prepare ahead
Yields 2 large loaves or 5 mini loaves

"This recipe makes a great Valentine treat for teachers because of its slightly pink tint."

3 cups all-purpose flour
1 teaspoon salt
1 teaspoon baking soda
1 tablespoon cinnamon
2 cups sugar
3 beaten eggs
1 1/4 cups vegetable oil
2 (10-ounce) boxes of frozen sliced
*   strawberries, thawed*
1 teaspoon vanilla extract
1 teaspoon almond extract

In a large mixing bowl, combine dry ingredients. Mix together beaten eggs and oil. Form a well in dry ingredients. Add eggs and oil. Mix well. Stir in strawberries, vanilla and almond extract. Pour into two well-greased 5x9-inch loaf pans or 5 mini-loaf pans. Bake at 350 degrees for 50 minutes. Allow to cool in pan before turning out.   —Josie Conner

Peel and mash overripe bananas and mix in a little lemon juice. Freeze in measured amounts. Thaw for making banana bread, cake or muffins

Broccoli Corn Bread

1 package chopped broccoli, thawed
2 cups sharp cheese, shredded
1/2 stick margarine
1 small package corn bread mix
4 eggs
1 medium onion, chopped

Combine all ingredients and mix well. Bake at 350 degrees for 45 minutes in a 9-inch rectangular pan.

—Lisa Thomas

Corn Bread

"This is a recipe shared by my cousin Sue Taylor from Farmville, N.C."

2 cups Bisquick (non-fat is fine)
1 stick margarine or I Can't Believe It's
*   Not Butter*
1 small can cream style corn

Melt margarine in Pyrex dish. Mix Bisquick and corn and knead. Shape to accommodate size of dish. Cut down the center. Cut across in finger-size pieces. Lift, roll in margarine and place in Pyrex dish. Bake 12 to 15 minutes at 450 degrees.

—Leslie Wallace

Easy Biscuits

Serve immediately
Yields 12–16 biscuits

1/3 cup canola oil
1/2 cup skim milk
1 1/2 cups self-rising flour

Preheat oven to 400 degrees. Pour oil into a four-cup measuring cup. Add the skim milk and flour. Mix with a fork until dough is moistened. Turn dough out onto a floured surface. Roll dough and cut with a biscuit cutter. Place biscuits on an ungreased cookie sheet and bake at 400 degrees for approximately 20 minutes.

—Sara Stowe

Apple Bread

May prepare ahead
Yields 2 loaves

1¹/₂ cups vegetable oil
2 cups sugar
3 cups all-purpose flour
3 eggs
1 teaspoon cinnamon
1 teaspoon salt
1 teaspoon baking soda
1 teaspoon vanilla extract
1 cup apple pie filling
1 cup nuts, chopped

Preheat oven to 350 degrees. Grease and flour two 5x9-inch loaf pans. Beat together oil, sugar, flour, eggs, cinnamon, salt, soda, and vanilla. Add apple pie filling and nuts. Pour into 2 loaf pans and bake for 1 hour at 350 degrees. Cool bread slightly in pans before turning out.

—Josie Conner

Big Batch Bran Muffins

May prepare ahead
Freezes well
Yields 5 dozen

3 cups sugar
1 cup vegetable oil
4 eggs
1 tablespoon plus 2 teaspoons
* baking soda*
1 tablespoon plus 1 teaspoon cinnamon
2 teaspoons salt
1 (17-ounce) can fruit cocktail,
* undrained*
5 cups all-purpose flour
1 quart buttermilk
1 (15-ounce) box Raisin Bran

Combine all ingredients and beat for 2 minutes on medium speed. Bake at 400 degrees for 16 to 18 minutes.

—Nannette Sylvester Anthony

To reheat bread or rolls, place in a paper bag, sprinkle the bag with water, and heat in a 400-degree oven for 10 minutes.

Doris's Sticky Buns

Serve immediately
Quick to prepare
Serves 10

"This recipe is a staple at our cottage. Saturday mornings and special occasion mornings wouldn't be complete without sticky buns. My good friend Doris Fowler, who lives in Canada, and is our 'neighbor' at the cottage, gave me this recipe about 8 years ago. They are so incredibly easy to make and convenient, especially if you prepare them the night before and let them rise overnight in the oven, yet taste like you've spent hours making them! They won't last long enough to even cool down!"

¹/₄ to ¹/₂ cup raisins
¹/₄ to ¹/₂ cup pecans, chopped (may also use walnuts or almonds)
2 loaves frozen bread dough or 1 package frozen white rolls, partially thawed
¹/₂ cup butter
1 cup brown sugar, packed
2 tablespoons milk
2 tablespoons cinnamon
1 large package vanilla pudding mix, not instant

Grease a 9x13-inch pan. Sprinkle desired amount of raisins and nuts over the bottom of the pan. Melt butter in a small bowl. Add brown sugar, milk, pudding mix and cinnamon. Mix thoroughly. Cut the bread dough into 1 inch pieces, if using frozen loaves, or break apart rolls, and place on top of raisins and nuts in the prepared pan. Pour brown sugar-pudding mixture over the bread. Let rise 2 hours in a warm place, or overnight in a cool oven, covered with wax paper. Bake at 375 degrees for 20 minutes. Turn upside down on an attractive platter to serve. Wonderful hot, right out of the oven!   —Barbara Emerson

To facilitate the final rising, place dough (which has been covered with a towel) in a cold oven with a pan of hot water on the bottom shelf.

Breakfast & Brunch

Bloody Mary

Must prepare ahead
Serves 6–8

Great for brunch!

1 (32-ounce) jar Beefomato juice
2 (6-ounce) cans Hot, Spicy V8
2 teaspoons Worcestershire sauce
2 cups vodka
several splashes Tabasco Sauce
lime to taste
dillweed to taste

Mix all of the ingredients together and let "perk" for 2 days (48 hours). These can be made and served immediately but are much better if they sit for 48 hours. "I have never served without letting them 'perk'!" —Cheryl Black

Champagne Punch

Serve chilled
Serve immediately
Serves 25

1 quart cranberry juice
1 quart orange juice
1 (2-liter) bottle ginger ale
1 bottle champagne

Chill all ingredients before mixing. Stir together cranberry and orange juices. Add ginger ale and champagne. Serve immediately.
—Betsy Forbes

Southern Almond Iced Tea

Serve chilled
Serves 10

1/2 gallon brewed tea
1/2 cup sugar
2 teaspoons almond extract
1 (6-ounce) can frozen lemonade
  concentrate
2 (12-ounce) bottles ginger ale

Mix tea, sugar and almond extract. Chill. Just before serving, add the lemonade concentrate and the ginger ale. —Josie Conner

Raspberry Punch

Serve chilled
May prepare ahead
Freezes well
Serves 10

1 quart raspberry sherbert, softened
2 (6-ounce) cans pink lemonade, slightly
*   thawed*
2 (28-ounce) bottles ginger ale

Mix all ingredients together and
chill.   —Susan B. Allen

Heavenly Dressing

Adaptable to low fat
May prepare ahead
Yields 2 cups

"Serve with fresh fruit. When
I received this recipe, it called
for whipped cream or sour cream.
Lately, I have substituted low
fat yogurt to lower the recipe's
fat grams and the dressing is
still good."

^{1}/2 cup sugar
2 tablespoons all-purpose flour
1 cup pineapple juice
1 egg, beaten
1 tablespoon margarine
1 cup whipping cream, whipped, or
*   1 cup yogurt or 1 cup sour cream*

Mix sugar and flour in a medium,
heavy-bottomed saucepan. Add
pineapple juice, egg and margarine
and cook over medium heat, stirring

constantly for about 5 minutes,
until the mixture thickens. Let cool
completely. Just before serving,
fold in the whipped cream.
          —Nan F. Bridgeman

Mango Fruit Parfaits

Serve chilled
Makes 4 large parfaits

2 cups mangos, cubed (about 2 mangos)
^{1}/4 cup orange juice, freshly squeezed
24 strawberries, hulled
1 cup kiwi, peeled and sliced (about
*   4 kiwis)*
12 red raspberries

Place the mangos and orange juice
in a blender and purée until smooth.
Slice 20 of the strawberries, leaving
4 whole. Line the bottom of 4
balloon wine glasses with the sliced
strawberries. Pour a thin layer of the
mango purée over each to cover.
Reserving four kiwi slices, layer the
remaining kiwi on top of the pureé.
Divide the remainder of the mango
purée among the four glasses. Top
each with a slice of kiwi surrounded
by raspberries. Make a slit in each of
the whole strawberries and position
one on the rim of each glass. Cover
and refrigerate for 15 minutes.
          —Heidi Latham

Piña Colada Fruit Dip

May prepare ahead
Yields 2½ cups

"This dip looks most tempting if served in a pineapple boat."

1 (8-ounce) can crushed pineapple in its
    own juice, undrained
1 (3.5-ounce) package instant coconut
    pudding and pie filling mix
¾ cup milk
½ cup dairy sour cream

Combine all ingredients in a food processor or a blender. Cover and process for 30 seconds. If using a blender, stir after 15 seconds. Refrigerate for several hours to blend flavors. Serve with fruit of choice.

—Robin Hackney

Applesauce

May prepare ahead
Freezes well
Low fat
Quick to prepare
Serves 6

6 cooking apples
1 cup water
¼ lemon, sliced
½ cup miniature marshmallows
¼ teaspoon mace
¼ teaspoon cinnamon
¼ teaspoon allspice

Wash and core apples. Put in a heavy pot with 1 cup of water and lemon slices. Cook on medium heat, stirring often, until the apples are saucy. Place in a sauce colander and strain. Add the marshmallows and spices. Mix well. Add additional marshmallows to sweeten; the amount depends on how sweet you like your applesauce and how tart the apples are. This applesauce can be served hot or cold.

—Mary Lu Leatherman

Summer Salad

Must prepare ahead
Serves 20

1 honeydew melon
2 cantaloupe melons
2 (20-ounce) cans pineapple chunks
2 (11-ounce) cans mandarin oranges,
    drained
1 (6-ounce) can frozen lemonade
    concentrate, thawed
¼ cup orange marmalade

Using a melon baller, make melon balls out of the honeydew and cantaloupes. In a large bowl, mix melon balls, pineapple, and oranges. In a small bowl, whisk together the lemonade concentrate and the orange marmalade. Pour the lemonade mixture over the fruit. Cover and chill several hours or overnight. Drain fruit and serve.

—Lucille Rinehart

Frozen Fruit Salad

Quick to prepare
Must prepare 1 day ahead
Freezes well
Serves 12–15

2 cups sugar
1 pint mayonnaise
1 pint whipping cream, whipped
8 ounces cheddar cheese, grated
2 (15-ounce) cans fruit cocktail,
    drained
1 (15-ounce) can chopped pears, drained
1 (15-ounce) can crushed pineapple,
    drained
6 bananas, sliced
3/4 cup toasted pecans

Mix all of the ingredients together
and pour into an 11x16 dish. Freeze
until frozen well. Cut into squares to
serve. Prepare 24 hours ahead.

—Jennifer Lynch

Fruit Casserole

Serves 10

"A Barkley Christmas Brunch
Tradition—Fruit Casserole,
Sausage Casserole and Applesauce
Cheese Biscuits."

1 (15-ounce) can peach halves
1 (15-ounce) can pineapple chunks
1 (15-ounce) can pear halves
1 (14-ounce) jar apple rings
2 tablespoons cornstarch
1/2 cup sherry
1/2 stick margarine
1/2 cup brown sugar, packed

Preheat oven to 350 degrees. Drain
fruit, reserving juices from peaches,
pineapple, and apple rings to equal
two cups. In a medium saucepan,
combine juices, cornstarch, sherry,
margarine, and brown sugar. Cook
over medium heat until mixture
thickens, stirring constantly. Place
fruit in a 9x13 pan and pour
thickened juice over top. Bake for
20 minutes.

—Laura Barkley-Thomas

*Dip your bananas in lemon juice right after they are peeled. They will not turn
dark and the faint flavor of lemon really adds to their flavor. The same may be
done with apples.*

Applesauce Cheese Biscuits

Freezes well
Makes 12 biscuits

2 cups all-purpose flour
2 teaspoons baking powder
1/4 teaspoon baking soda
1 teaspoon salt
4 tablespoons shortening
3/4 cup applesauce
3/4 cup sharp cheddar cheese, grated

Sift together dry ingredients. Cut in shortening until it looks like fine bread crumbs. Add applesauce and grated cheese. Stir with fork until mixed. Roll out the dough and cut to desired size. Bake at 400 degrees for 15 minutes.

—Laura Barkley-Thomas

Breakfast Cookies

May prepare ahead
Freezes well

1 cup all-purpose flour, unsifted
3/4 cup sugar
1/4 teaspoon baking soda
1/2 cup bacon, crumbled
1/2 cup margarine
1 egg
2 cups Corn Flakes cereal

Mix flour, sugar, baking soda and crumbled bacon. Add margarine and egg. Mix well. Stir in cereal. Drop by spoonfuls about 1 inch apart on an ungreased cookie sheet. Bake at 350 degrees for 13 to 15 minutes until slightly brown but still soft.

—Mary Lu Leatherman

Susan's Breakfast Bites

Serves 30–45

2 cups Bisquick
3/4 cup lean ham, chopped
1 cup sharp cheddar cheese, grated
1/2 cup Parmesan cheese, grated
1/2 cup onion, finely chopped
2 tablespoons fresh, snipped parsley
1/2 teaspoon salt
2 garlic cloves, crushed
1/4 cup sour cream
2/3 cup milk
1 egg

Preheat oven to 350 degrees. Grease a 9x13-inch baking pan. In a large mixing bowl, combine Bisquick, ham, cheeses, onion, parsley, salt and garlic. Beat together sour cream, milk and egg. Add to dry ingredients and mix until moistened. Spread in pan. Bake for 25 to 30 minutes or until golden brown. Let cool in pan. Cut into sixty 1-inch squares.

—Susan Absher

Grandma Friesen's Spoon Bread

Serve immediately
Serves 6–8

"Our family has many fond memories of waking up to the smells of my Grandmother's spoon bread, eggs and sausage cooking in the kitchen. It always seemed to bring a smile to our faces."

2 cups yellow corn meal
2 tablespoons baking powder
1 tablespoon salt
4 cups water
5 eggs, beaten
2 cups water
4 tablespoons vegetable oil

Mix the first three ingredients in a large pot on the stove. Stir into corn meal mixture the 4 cups of water and bring to a boil. Blend the eggs into the mixture. Add the 2 cups of water and 4 tablespoons oil to the corn meal mixture. Cook slowly, constantly stirring. Bring to a boil again and cook for approximately 5 minutes. Preheat oven to 500 degrees allowing a Pyrex pan with approximately 2 tablespoons oil in it to preheat as well. Add the cooked corn meal mixture to the heated pan. Be careful not to get burned by the spattering of hot oil. Reduce oven to 450 degrees and bake for 25 to 40 minutes or until lightly brown around the edges.   —Shelly Carter

Baked Peach French Toast

Serve immediately
Serves 6

10 to 14 slices French bread, cut in one
*   inch thick slices*
1 (3-ounce) package cream cheese,
*   softened*
1 (29-ounce) can sliced peaches, drained
1/4 cup nuts, chopped
1 cup milk
1/3 cup maple syrup
3 eggs
1 tablespoon sugar
1 teaspoon ground cinnamon
1 teaspoon vanilla extract

Preheat oven to 400 degrees. Spread cream cheese on both sides of bread slices. Place slices in a 9x13-inch baking dish. Prick the top of each slice with a fork several times, and top with peach slices. Sprinkle nuts over peaches. Combine the remaining ingredients in a bowl and whisk. Pour egg mixture over the bread. Bake 20 to 30 minutes or until the mixture is set.

—Betse Huston

You may determine the age of an egg by placing it in the bottom of a bowl of cold water. If it stays on its side, it is very fresh. If it stands at an angle, it is at least 3 days old. If it stands on end, it is at least 10 days old.

Norwegian Kringler

Serves 20

1 tablespoon water
1 cup all-purpose flour
1 tablespoon sugar
1/2 cup margarine or butter
1 cup water
1/2 cup margarine or butter
1 cup all-purpose flour
1 tablespoon sugar
1/2 teaspoon almond extract
3 eggs
1 cup confectioners' sugar
1 tablespoon half-and-half
1 tablespoon margarine or butter
2 to 3 teaspoons almond extract

In a medium bowl, combine 1 tablespoon water, 1 cup flour, 1 tablespoon sugar and 1/2 cup margarine. Mix with a fork until it is the size of small peas. Form the dough into a ball and divide in half. On an ungreased cookie sheet, form the dough into two 3x14-inch rectangles. Prepare the topping in a medium saucepan by heating 1 cup water and 1/2 cup margarine to a boil. Remove from heat. Add 1 cup flour and stir until smooth. Beat in 1 tablespoon sugar and almond extract. Add eggs, one at a time, beating well after each addition. Spread the topping mixture over the dough rectangles. Bake at 375 degrees for 30 to 35 minutes. To make the glaze, combine the confectioners' sugar, half-and-half, 1 tablespoon margarine and almond extract. Drizzle over cooled kringler.   —Vicky Heinrich

Old Fashioned Stickies

Serve immediately
Yields 9–12 stickies

"This recipe is from my great-grandmother. This recipe differs from York County Stickies."

2 cups all-purpose flour
1 teaspoon baking powder
1/2 teaspoon baking soda
1 teaspoon salt
3 tablespoons shortening
buttermilk to make soft dough
1 1/2 sticks margarine, softened
3/4 cup sugar
1 small can evaporated milk
1 teaspoon vanilla extract

Mix flour, baking powder, soda and salt. Cut in shortening until mixture resembles coarse meal. Add buttermilk to make soft dough. Roll out thin. Spread with margarine and sprinkle with sugar. Roll the dough into an oblong roll and cut into slices 3/4 to 1 inch wide. Place slices, cut side up, in 9 inch cake pans. Dilute evaporated milk with 1/2 can of water and add vanilla. Pour the milk mixture over the dough rolls. Bake at 400 degrees until golden brown.

—Lindsay Lockett

"Little Grandma's" Maple Nut Ring

Serve immediately
Quick to prepare
Serves 8

"Although embarrassingly simple to make, this dish will bring rave reviews from all who try it!"

¹/₂ cup margarine
¹/₃ cup brown sugar, packed
¹/₂ cup nuts, chopped
¹/₄ cup maple syrup
1 teaspoon cinnamon
2 (10-ounce) cans biscuits

In a saucepan, melt the margarine. Stir in brown sugar, nuts, cinnamon, and syrup. Pour ¹/₄ cup of the mixture into a lightly greased fluted tube pan. Stand separated biscuits on edge, slightly overlapping around the pan. Pour the remaining mixture over the biscuits. Bake at 350 degrees for 25 to 35 minutes or until golden brown. Cool for 3 minutes; invert onto a serving plate. —Shelly Carter

Sally's Stuffed French Toast

Prepare ahead
Serves 8–10

8 slices firm, white toasting bread
2 (8-ounce) packages cream cheese, softened
1 dozen eggs, beaten
2 cups milk
¹/₂ cup pure maple syrup

Trim and cube the eight slices of bread. Place half of the bread in the bottom of a 9x13 casserole dish. Cube the cream cheese and put it on top of the bread. Then put the rest of the bread on top of the cream cheese. Add the milk to the beaten eggs. Mix well. Add the syrup and mix well; pour on top of the bread and cream cheese. Cover and refrigerate overnight. Bake at 375 degrees for 45 minutes. Serve with additional syrup.   —Mary Randall Rhyne

Quick and Easy Apple Dumplings

Serve immediately
Serves 6

3 apples, peeled and cut in quarters
1 (6-count) can biscuits
1 tablespoon sugar
cinnamon to taste
1 cup water
1 stick butter or margarine, melted

Preheat oven to 350 degrees. Separate each biscuit to form two rounds. Place one apple quarter in the center of each round. Sprinkle with sugar and cinnamon. Stretch biscuit round over the apple and pinch to seal. Pour water into a baking dish. Place dumplings in the dish with the water. Pour the melted butter over the top of the dumplings. Sprinkle the tops of the dumplings with extra sugar and cinnamon. Bake for 20 minutes.   —Holt A. Harris

"Little Grandma's" Danish Puff

Refrigerate before serving
Serves 6–8
Yields 2 Danish strips

"This has become a Christmas morning treat for our family introduced to us by my grandmother, Newell Nunn."

Danish Puffs:
1 cup all-purpose flour
1/2 cup butter
2 tablespoons water

Preheat oven to 350 degrees.
In a mixing bowl, place flour. Cut in butter until the mixture is crumbly. Add water and mix with a fork. Round the dough into a ball and divide the ball in half. Pat each half into a strip and place on an ungreased baking sheet.

Creme Center:
1/2 cup butter
1 cup water
1 teaspoon vanilla extract
1 cup all-purpose flour
3 eggs

In a saucepan, bring the butter and water to a boil. Remove from heat and stir in the vanilla. Beat in the flour, stirring quickly to prevent lumping. When the mixture is smooth, add one unbeaten egg at a time, beating well after each addition. Pour half of the mixture on one pastry strip and the other half on the other strip. Bake until the tops are puffed and lightly brown, approximately 30 to 40 minutes. Check frequently so the danish puffs do not get too brown.

Icing:
3 tablespoons butter, softened
2 tablespoons warm milk
2 cups confectioners' sugar
1/2 teaspoon vanilla extract
chopped pecans, optional

While the danish puffs are baking, place the butter and milk for the icing in a bowl on the stove so they can warm. Mix in confectioners' sugar and vanilla. If the icing is too thick, add 1/2 to 1 tablespoon more milk. When the danish puffs are through baking, frost the tops with the icing and sprinkle with chopped pecans, if desired. Refrigerate until ready to serve.   —Shelly Carter

Delicious Pasta Salad

Serve chilled
May prepare ahead
Serves 12–14

1 (16-ounce) bottle zesty Italian
 dressing
1 (16-ounce) box linguine, broken into
 fourths
1/4 cup Salad Supreme Seasoning Spice
1 large tomato, chopped
1 cucumber, peeled and chopped
1 tablespoon poppy seeds
1 tablespoon sunflower seeds
1 tablespoon sesame seeds
2 to 3 green onions, sliced

Cook the linguine according to the
directions on the box, but remove
from the stove before getting too
soft. Rinse and drain pasta, then stir
in the remaining ingredients. Chill.

—Susan Allen

Pecan and Crumbled Cheese Salad

Serves 8

1 head red leaf lettuce
1 head bib or butter lettuce
1/2 small red bell pepper, chopped
1/2 small green bell pepper, chopped
1 small purple onion, sliced thin
1 large tomato, very ripe and cut into
 chunks
3/4 cup pecans, chopped
1 tablespoon basil, finely sliced or
 1/2 tablespoon dried basil
1/4 teaspoon oregano
salt and pepper to taste
2/3 cup olive oil
2 tablespoons balsamic vinegar (may
 add minced garlic to vinegar, if
 desired)
1 package crumbled bleu or feta cheese

Wash lettuce well and pat dry. Tear
lettuce into bite size pieces and put
in a large salad bowl. Add peppers,
onion, tomato, pecans, and spices.
Toss well. Sprinkle with crumbled
cheese. Add olive oil and vinegar.
Toss and serve.   —Denise Smith

Asparagus Cheese Strata

Prepare one day ahead
Serves 10–12

1 1/2 pounds fresh asparagus, cut into
  2-inch pieces
3 tablespoons butter or margarine,
  melted
1 loaf sliced white bread, crusts removed
3/4 cup cheddar cheese, shredded and
  divided
2 cups ham or turkey, cooked and cubed
6 eggs
3 cups milk
2 teaspoons minced onion
1/2 teaspoon salt
1/4 teaspoon dry mustard

Cook the asparagus in water until it
is tender yet still firm. Drain. Brush
butter on one side of bread slices.
Place half of the bread buttered side
up in a greased 9x13-inch baking
dish. Sprinkle with 1/2 cup of cheese.
Layer with asparagus and meat.
Cover with the remaining bread.
Beat eggs, milk, onion, salt and
mustard and pour over the bread.
Refrigerate overnight. Bake
uncovered at 325 degrees for 50
minutes. Sprinkle with remaining
cheese. Cook 10 more minutes or
until the cheese is melted.

—Janice Stowe

Herbed Stuffed Snow Peas

May prepare ahead
Serves 8

2 pounds snow peas, fresh or frozen
8 ounces cream cheese, softened
8 ounces sour cream
1 package Good Seasons Italian
  dressing, dry
6 cups boiling water, salted

Cream together cream cheese, sour
cream and dry Italian dressing mix
until blended and creamy. Set aside
at room temperature. Place snow
peas in a large bowl. Slowly pour
salted, boiling water over the peas.
Let stand for 3 to 5 minutes. Rinse
with cold water. Drain and pat
dry. Cut the string side of the pea
completely off and open the pea.
Place the cream cheese mixture in
a large pastry bag fitted with a
decorative tip. Pipe the mixture
into the peas. Chill.   —Amy Boyd

A little salt added to eggs while beating
will speed up the process.

Breakfast Tortilla Torta

Prepare ahead
Serves 12

"Kaye Adams made this for our Circle Brunch at her beautiful lake home in 1995. It was wonderful!"

3 teaspoons olive oil
1 pound new potatoes, thinly sliced
8 green onions, sliced
1 teaspoon chili powder
1/2 teaspoon salt
3 eggs
3 egg whites
1 cup whole kernel corn, drained
2/3 dash pepper
1 pound hot sausage
1 sweet red pepper, finely chopped
5 flour tortillas, 10 inch size
1/2 cup cheddar cheese, shredded
sour cream
salsa

Preheat oven to 400 degrees. Coat a 10 inch springform pan with non-stick spray and set aside. In a skillet, heat the oil over medium heat. Add the potatoes and cook, stirring occasionally, for 12 minutes or until tender. Add 1/3 cup of the green onions, chili powder and 1/4 teaspoon of the salt. Cook for 2 additional minutes. Pour into a bowl. Coat another skillet with non-stick spray. Beat eggs, egg whites (may use 6 whole eggs), corn, pepper and remaining salt. Cook over medium heat for 2 to 3 minutes or just until set, stirring constantly. Pour into another bowl. Brown sausage with red pepper and remaining green onions. Cook about 6 minutes or until no longer pink, breaking up sausage. Drain well. Stir in 1/4 cup salsa. To assemble torta, place tortilla in the bottom of the springform pan. Spoon on potato mixture, spreading evenly. Top with tortilla, pressing flat. Spoon on half of sausage mixture, spreading evenly. Top with tortilla, egg mixture, tortilla, remaining sausage mixture, tortilla. Spoon on a layer of salsa. Sprinkle with shredded cheese. Bake for 40 minutes or until the egg mixture is set, tenting loosely with aluminun foil during last 20 minutes. Let stand 10 minutes before serving. Serve with sour cream and salsa.

Note: The potato and sausage mixtures can be prepared the night before to save time!

—Eva Ann McLean

Breakfast Shrimp with Grits

Quick to prepare
Serves 8

3 cups raw shrimp, peeled
4 tablespoons onion, chopped
4 teaspoons green bell pepper, chopped
6 tablespoons bacon drippings
salt and pepper to taste
2 teaspoons Worcestershire sauce
2 tablespoons ketchup
3 tablespoons all-purpose flour
1 (10³/4-ounce) can cream of
  mushroom soup
shot of sherry
1 cup water

Combine onion, green pepper and
bacon drippings in a frying pan.
Cook until onions are golden brown.
Add shrimp. Cook for 3 minutes,
stirring often. Add enough water to
make a sauce, about 1 cup. Cook 2
more minutes. Combine flour with
just enough water to make a paste.
Add to the shrimp mixture. Add
seasonings and sherry. Cook until
thickened. Serve over grits.

—Mrs. Joseph S. Stowe

Almond-Topped Crab Quiche

Serve immediately
Serves 6–8

1 (9-inch) deep-dish pie shell
¹/2 teaspoon salt
1 cup Swiss cheese, grated
¹/2 teaspoon lemon rind, grated
¹/2 pound fresh crab meat
dash of dry mustard
2 green onions, sliced
dash of black pepper
3 eggs
¹/4 cup sliced almonds
1 cup half-and-half

In a preheated 400-degree oven,
bake the pie shell for 3 minutes.
Remove from oven and gently prick
with a fork. Bake 5 minutes longer
and let cool. Sprinkle cheese evenly
in the cooled shell. Place crab meat
on top of cheese, followed by green
onions. Beat eggs until foamy; stir in
half-and-half, salt, lemon rind, dry
mustard and pepper. Pour the egg
mixture into the pie shell and
sprinkle with almonds. Bake at 325
degrees for 1 hour or until set. Let
stand for 10 minutes before serving.

—Amy Black

Crab Quiche

Serve immediately
Serves 8

2 eggs, beaten
¹/2 cup milk
¹/2 cup mayonnaise
2 teaspoons all-purpose flour
8 ounces Swiss cheese, shredded
2 (6.25-ounce) cans crab meat, drained and rinsed
1 small onion, chopped
1 frozen deep dish pie shell
dash of salt and pepper

Beat together eggs and milk. Mix the flour and mayonnaise. Add to the eggs and milk. Stir in the cheese, crab meat, onion, salt and pepper. Pour into the pie shell. Bake at 350 degrees for 45 minutes. Let cool 10 minutes before cutting.

—Lisa Thomas

Ham and Broccoli Quiche

May prepare ahead
Serves 6–8

4 eggs, beaten
1¹/2 cups milk
1 teaspoon salt, can use less
1 teaspoon dry mustard
¹/2 teaspoon pepper
1 package chopped broccoli, thawed
1 cup ham, chopped
1¹/2 cups cheddar cheese, grated
2 deep-dish pie shells, cooked

Combine eggs, milk, salt, mustard and pepper. Pour over broccoli, ham and cheese and blend well. Pour mixture into baked pie shells. Bake at 375 degrees for 30 minutes.

—Pam Paige

Garden Scramble

Low fat
Serves 2

1 (8-ounce) carton egg substitute
¹/8 teaspoon black pepper
¹/8 teaspoon marjoram leaves, optional
¹/4 cup celery, finely chopped
¹/4 cup red bell pepper, finely chopped
2 tablespoons green bell pepper, finely chopped
1 tablespoon chives, chopped
1 (16-ounce) can fat-free chicken broth
1 cup non-fat cheddar cheese, grated
low-fat whole wheat bread, toasted

In a bowl, combine egg substitute, pepper, and marjoram. Set aside. In a non-stick skillet sprayed with non-fat cooking spray, cook the celery, red pepper, green pepper, and chives in chicken broth over medium heat until tender. Add the egg substitute and grated cheese to the mixture. Cook, stirring occasionally until set. Serve immediately over toast halves if desired, or serve plain.

—Holt A. Harris

Sausage and Grits Casserole

Must prepare ahead
Serves 6–8

2 cups water
1/2 teaspoon salt
1/2 cup quick cooking grits
1 cup milk
4 cups cheddar cheese, shredded
4 eggs, beaten
1/2 teaspoon thyme
1/8 teaspoon garlic salt
2 pounds hot or mild sausage, cooked
  and crumbled

Bring water and salt to a boil. Stir in grits. Cook for 4 minutes. Add milk and cheese and stir until melted. Mix eggs, thyme and garlic salt. Add a small amount of grits mixture and stir well. Then stir egg mixture back into all of grits. Add the sausage. Pour into a greased 9x13 inch baking dish. Refrigerate overnight. Remove from refrigerator and let stand for fifteen minutes. Bake at 350 degrees for 50 to 55 minutes.

—Mrs. Joseph S. Stowe

Petite Tomato Pies

Must prepare one day ahead
Serves 16

"Wonderful for bridal or baby shower luncheons or for large family gatherings."

16 individual size tart shells
5 fresh tomatoes
1/2 teaspoon salt
3 teaspoons basil
2 teaspoons garlic powder
1 1/4 cups sharp cheddar cheese, grated
3/4 cup mayonnaise

Peel and cut tomatoes into small cubes. Add the salt, basil and garlic powder. Marinate overnight. Drain thoroughly. Cook tart shells according to the directions on the package. Remove when slightly brown and let cool completely. Fill the cooled shells with the tomato mixture. Mix the cheese and mayonnaise. Spoon this mixture over the pies. Bake at 350 degrees until brown.

—Laura Calhoun Dixon

When cooking oatmeal, coat the kettle with nonstick cooking spray. It keeps the oatmeal from boiling over and sticking to the kettle.

Blue Ribbon Trifle

Refrigerate before serving
Serves 10

1½ cups lowfat Pioneer baking mix
4 tablespoons cocoa
2 (8-ounce) cartons chocolate almond
    yogurt
1 tablespoon vanilla extract
¼ cup canned skim milk
1 egg

Toppings:

1 large box sugarless instant vanilla
    pudding, prepared according to
    package directions
1 large box sugarless instant chocolate
    pudding, prepared according to
    package directions
2 tablespoons vanilla extract
1 (12-ounce) container frozen whipped
    topping, thawed
¼ cup pecans, crushed, optional

Preheat oven to 350 degrees. Spray a 9x13 pan with non-stick cooking spray. In a large mixing bowl, combine baking mix, cocoa, yogurt, vanilla, milk and egg. Spread cake batter in a thin layer in the pan. Bake for 10 minutes. Let cool. Break cooled cake apart and place in the bottom of a 9x12 serving dish. For the toppings, add 1 tablespoon of the vanilla to prepared vanilla pudding and stir well. Add the remaining 1 tablespoon vanilla to prepared chocolate pudding and stir well. Layer the chocolate pudding over the cake. Layer the vanilla pudding over the chocolate pudding. Spread the thawed whipped topping on top. Sprinkle with crushed pecans, if desired. Refrigerate and serve.

—Susan Allen

For tastier pancakes, add 1 tablespoon of pancake syrup to the batter.

Refreshing Cranberry Parfaits

Must prepare ahead
Makes 10–12 servings

"My mother, Kay Friesen, has made this wonderful dessert for as long as I can remember. You will be surprised at how many times you will be asked for the recipe."

2 (1-pound) cans jellied cranberry sauce
4 tablespoons confectioners' sugar
2 egg whites, stiffly beaten
2 cups heavy cream, whipped
2 teaspoons almond extract
1 cup toasted almonds

Using a fork, beat the cranberry sauce and sugar together. Do not mix until smooth. Allow small chunks to remain. Fold in the beaten egg whites, whipped cream and almond extract. Place the bowl in the freezer and allow mixture to become almost firm. Beat with a fork and put into parfait glasses. Return to the freezer to finish freezing. Sprinkle the parfaits with toasted almonds before serving.

—Shelly Carter

Cherry Bourbon Ice Cream

Must prepare 1 day ahead
Serves 12–14

1/2 gallon vanilla ice cream
2 dozen almond macaroons, or plain macaroons with a few drops of almond extract
1 can pitted Bing cherries, cut up, juice saved
1/2 cup bourbon
1 cup pecans, chopped

Soak the cherries, with the juice, overnight in 1/2 cup of bourbon and 1 cup of chopped pecans. Soften the ice cream. Crush the macaroons. Mix the crumbs and cherry mixture with the ice cream. Refreeze in dessert dishes or in bulk.

—Emily Simpson

Soups & Stews

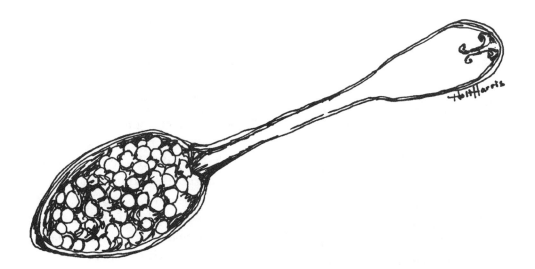

Baked Potato Soup

Serve immediately
Serves 10–12

4 large baking potatoes
12 slices bacon, cooked and crumbled
2/3 cup butter or margarine
2/3 cup all-purpose flour
1 1/4 cup shredded cheddar cheese
6 cups milk
3/4 teaspoon salt
1 (8-ounce) carton sour cream
1/2 teaspoon pepper
4 green onions, chopped

Wash and prick potatoes. Bake at 400 degrees for 1 hour. Let cool. Cut in half lengthwise. Scoop out pulp and set aside. Discard skins. Melt butter in heavy saucepan over low heat. Add flour, stirring until smooth. Cook 1 minute, stirring constantly. Gradually add milk. Cook over medium heat, stirring constantly, until thick and bubbly. Add potato pulp, green onions, bacon, salt and cheese. Heat thoroughly. Stir in sour cream. Add extra milk for desired thickness. Garnish with sour cream, green onions or cheese.   —Susan Allen

White Chili

May prepare ahead
Freezes well
Serves 4–6

4 chicken breasts
2 (15 1/2-ounce) cans white beans,
     drained
1 teaspoon lemon juice
1 teaspoon cumin
2 (4-ounce) cans green chilies
1 tablespoon olive oil
1 garlic clove, chopped
2 (9-ounce) packages frozen white corn
1 cup onion, chopped

Cook the chicken breasts in water to cover and reserve 1 1/2 cups of the broth. Chop the chicken and add it back to the reserved broth, along with all the other ingredients. Cook slowly over low heat to enhance flavor. Sprinkle with Monterey Jack cheese. Serve with tortillas.

—Julie Fleming

To degrease soup, spread a paper towel across the surface of the soup to absorb some of the grease or refrigerate the soup. The fat will harden at the surface and can be lifted off easily.

Broccoli Cheese Soup

Freezes well
Serves 12

"This is a family favorite from my Mom's collection of special recipes."

2 tablespoons vegetable oil
$^1/_8$ teaspoon garlic powder
$^3/_4$ cup onion, chopped
6 cups milk
6 cups water
1 pound Velveeta cheese spread
6 chicken bouillon cubes
1 (8-ounce) package fine egg noodles or
    thin spaghetti
2 (10-ounce) packages chopped frozen
    broccoli
salt and pepper to taste

Heat oil in large saucepan. Sauté onion over medium heat for three minutes. Add water and bouillon cubes. Bring to a boil. Cook, stirring occasionally, until bouillon cubes dissolve. Gradually add egg noodles and salt and continue to boil. Cook for 3 minutes, stirring often. Stir in broccoli and garlic powder and cook 4 more minutes. Add milk, cheese and pepper to taste. Continue cooking until cheese melts.

—Leslie Wallace

Sweet and Sour Cabbage Soup

Freezes well
Serves 10–15

"This very unusual and delicious soup is one of my favorite soups served at Covenant Village Retirement Community."

1 pound ground beef
1 large head cabbage, shredded
1 large onion, chopped
3 quarts water
$^1/_4$ cup lemon juice
1 beef bouillon cube
$^1/_2$ cup cider vinegar
$^1/_2$ teaspoon white pepper
6 ounces sugar
1 can crushed tomatoes

Brown the ground beef and onion. Pour off grease. Bring water to a boil. Add bouillon cube, pepper, tomatoes and shredded cabbage to the boiling water. Bring to a boil. Reduce heat to medium. Add lemon juice, vinegar and sugar to simmering soup. Cook for 15 to 20 minutes.

—Julie Heath

Cauliflower Soup

Serve immediately
Serves 6

1 medium head cauliflower, broken into
    small pieces
2 cups half-and-half
2/3 cup onion, finely chopped
1/2 teaspoon Worcestershire sauce
1/2 stick butter
2 tablespoons all-purpose flour
grated cheddar cheese
2 cups chicken broth
fresh cut chives
salt to taste

Cover cauliflower with salted water.
Boil until tender, drain and save
liquid. In large pot, melt butter
over low heat. Add onion and sauté.
Stir in flour and cook for 2 minutes.
Blend in chicken broth. Cook
over medium-high heat, stirring
constantly, until mixture boils. Add
1 cup cauliflower liquid, half-and-
half, salt and Worcestershire sauce.
Add cooked cauliflower. Before
serving, heat soup to boiling, remove
from heat and stir in grated cheese
to taste. Ladle into bowls and
sprinkle more cheese and fresh cut
chives over top.

—Laura Calhoun Dixon

Sweet Potato Soup

Yields 10 (6-ounce) servings

"No loss of fat grams here, but
people love it!"

2 large cans yams
2 cups water
2 chicken bouillon cubes
2 teaspoons ground cinnamon
1 stick butter, melted
1 quart half-and-half

Combine the butter with the
bouillon cubes, stirring to dissolve
the bouillon cubes. Bring water to
a boil; add to butter mixture. Add
yams and cinnamon, simmering
slowly to blend flavors. Slowly add
half and half, stirring often. Serve
hot or cold. Looks nice presented in
wine goblets as a cold soup.

—Anne Malonee

Supper Club Gazpacho

May prepare ahead
Serve chilled
Serves 6

1 (10³/4-ounce) can tomato soup
2 tablespoons Italian dressing
1¹/2 cups tomato juice
1 tablespoon lemon juice
1¹/4 cups water
1 garlic clove, minced
1 cup cucumber, chopped
1/4 teaspoon pepper
1 cup tomato, chopped
1/4 teaspoon hot sauce
1/2 cup green bell pepper, chopped
1/2 tablespoon wine vinegar

Combine ingredients and chill for
6 hours.   —Beth Brittain

Soup for the Slopes

Serve immediately
Serves 8–12

"This is a great soup for a cold
winter day! My mother used to
make this soup in a cast iron
kettle in our fireplace to be ready
just in time for a Carolina
basketball game!"

1 pound sausage, cooked and drained
1 cup potatoes, uncooked and diced
1/2 teaspoon seasoning salt
2 (16-ounce) cans kidney beans
1/2 teaspoon garlic salt
1 (28-ounce) can tomatoes
1/2 teaspoon thyme
1/2 onion, chopped
1/2 teaspoon pepper
1 quart water
1 bay leaf
1/2 green bell pepper, chopped

Mix kidney beans, tomatoes, onion,
spices and water. Simmer 1 hour.
Add sausage, potatoes and green
pepper. Simmer 20 minutes or until
vegetables are tender.
                    —Leslie Wallace

If soup tastes very salty, a raw piece of potato placed in the pot will absorb some
of the salt.

Black Bean Soup

Yields 20 (6-ounce) servings

1/2 cup onion, diced
2 (15-ounce) cans black beans,
  rinsed, drained
2 garlic cloves, chopped
1/4 cup olive oil
1/3 cup sugar
1/2 cup celery, diced
1 cup white wine
2 cups white rice, cooked
2 cups water
1 (46-ounce) can V-8 juice
2 tablespoons jalapeño pepper, diced
2 (28-ounce) cans diced tomatoes,
  undrained
1/2 cup fresh torn cilantro

Sauté onion and garlic in olive oil. Add celery and sauté until soft. Combine all other ingredients except cilantro and simmer until flavors are blended, about 45 minutes. Just before removing from heat, add cilantro.   —Anne Malonee

Gourmet Chicken Soup

Serve immediately
Freezes well
Serves 8–10

4 large chicken breasts, with skin
  and bones
1 (10-ounce) box frozen, cut green beans
12 to 16 cups water
salt and pepper to taste
1 cup converted rice, uncooked
1 cup sour cream
1 (10-ounce) box frozen, chopped
  spinach

In a large pot, place the chicken breasts in water. Bring to a boil, reduce heat and simmer until chicken is thoroughly cooked. Remove chicken and let cool. Remove the skin and bones and chop the meat into bite sized pieces. Chill broth and skim off fat. Bring broth to a boil, add rice and cook until rice is tender. Add chicken, frozen vegetables and seasoning. Cook until vegetables are tender. Stir in sour cream immediately before serving.   —Lucille Rinehart

Muddle-Fish Stew

Serve immediately
Serves 4

"I had looked for a good recipe for years for fish stew. This one, from Chef Bill Neal of the Outer Banks, is wonderful!"

5 slices bacon
1 dried chili pepper
4 yellow onions, quartered and sliced
6 ounces white fish, skinless, boneless, non-oily
3/4 cup celery, finely chopped
1 teaspoon garlic, minced
6 ounces shrimp, peeled and deveined
1/2 teaspoon orange zest, finely grated
1 3/4 pounds tomatoes, undrained
6 ounces bay scallops or sea scallops, quartered
1 pound red waxy potatoes, peeled, cut into 1/2-inch cubes
1/2 cup green onions, finely chopped (including tops)
5 cups stock, fish or shrimp
1 1/2 tablespoons fresh basil, finely chopped
6 sprigs fresh thyme, or 1/2 teaspoon dried thyme
salt to taste
1 1/2 tablespoons fresh parsley, finely chopped

In a large pot over medium-high heat, cook the bacon until crisp and rendered of fat. Remove to paper towels and set aside. Add the onions, celery, garlic and orange zest to the bacon fat in the pot. Reduce the heat to low and simmer, stirring for 2 minutes. Add the tomatoes and cook two minutes longer. Add the potatoes, fish stock, thyme, dried chili pepper and salt. Stir well. Cover pot and simmer until the potatoes are tender but not mushy, about 20 minutes. Add the fish and shrimp and simmer uncovered for one minute. Stir in the scallops and cook 1 minute longer. Add more salt to taste and remove from heat. Remove and discard the dried chili pepper. In a small bowl, combine the crumbled bacon, green onions, basil and parsley. To serve, ladle the stew into individual bowls and garnish with bacon mixture. If you are unable to find red snapper or grouper, orange roughy works well.

—Eva Ann McLean

If soups or sauces with tomatoes are too acidic, add a little sugar to cut down on the acidic taste.

Bobby's Venison Stew

Serve immediately
Serves 8

2 pounds venison, cut in 1-inch cubes
1/4 cup bacon drippings
water
1 1/2 teaspoons salt
1/2 teaspoon black pepper
1 teaspoon garlic salt
1 teaspoon Worcestershire sauce
3/4 cup onion, chopped
4 medium potatoes, cubed
6 medium carrots, sliced
1 green bell pepper, chopped
2 cups celery, sliced
3 tablespoons all-purpose flour
1/4 cup cold water

Sauté venison in bacon drippings in heavy Dutch oven, turning to brown all sides of meat. Add water to cover, seasonings and onion. Simmer, covered, about 2 hours. Add vegetables and cook about 20 minutes, or until vegetables are tender. Dissolve flour in 1/4 cup water and stir into stew; cook about 5 minutes. Serve hot.

—Kelley L. Wright

Cheese Soup

Serves 6–8

"This is a family recipe that was shared by many on those cold Christmas Eve dinners in Pennsylvania. The pot was always empty!"

1/2 pound bacon, cooked and crumbled,
    save bacon drippings
1 cup celery, chopped
1 cup green bell pepper, chopped
1 cup onion, chopped
1 cup carrots, chopped
1 cup potatoes, chopped
1/4 cup all-purpose flour
6 cups low-sodium beef or chicken broth,
    or a combination
4 cups shredded Old English cheese or
    2 cups Old English and
    2 cups Velveeta

Sauté vegetables in bacon drippings in a large pot for approximately 20 minutes. Add flour and mix. Add broth and cheese. Simmer over low heat until cheese melts. Stir in bacon.

—Alice Krawczyk

To enhance the flavor of homemade vegetable soup, add chicken or beef bouillon cubes to the stock.

Salads &
Dressings

Bleu Cheese Dressing

Serve immediately
Yields: 3 cups

8 ounces crumbled bleu cheese
2 cups mayonnaise
2/3 cup milk
1/2 teaspoon celery seed
1/4 teaspoon garlic powder
1/4 teaspoon onion powder
dash of red pepper

Blend all ingredients except bleu cheese. Add crumbled bleu cheese and blend by hand. Thin with milk.

—Merryman Cleveland

Fresh Spinach Salad Dressing

May prepare ahead
Yields: 2 cups

"This recipe was given to me by my mother, Gretina T. Vaughn."

1/2 cup vinegar
1/2 cup sugar
1 cup oil
1/3 cup ketchup
1 medium onion, cut into eighths

Place vinegar, sugar, oil, ketchup and onion in blender. Blend until onion is finely chopped and ingredients are blended. Pour over a spinach salad.

—Cherry Howe

House Dressing

Must prepare 1 day ahead
Yields: 2 cups

1/2 cup fresh parsley
1 cup carrots
1/2 cup buttermilk
1 1/2 cups mayonnaise
3/4 teaspoon garlic powder
1/4 teaspoon garlic salt
1/4 teaspoon salt

Chop parsley and carrots finely. May use cuisinart but do not over chop. Combine remaining ingredients until smooth. Stir in carrots and parsley. Cover and refrigerate overnight. Delicious on fresh baby greens.

—Shelby S. Rhyne

Hot Lettuce Salad Dressing

Serve immediately
Yields: 2¹/2 cups

¹/2 pound bacon cut in small pieces
2 eggs
¹/2 cup sugar
¹/2 cup white vinegar
¹/2 cup water

Fry bacon; set aside. Save grease from bacon. Mix remaining ingredients together in separate bowl. Place pan with bacon grease back on the stove (medium heat). Slowly add the combined ingredients to the heated grease. Bring to a slow boil and continue to boil for 2 minutes. Add cooked bacon. Serve over mixed greens.　　—Alice Krawczyk

Cheddar Cheese Salad Dressing

May prepare ahead
Yields: 2¹/2 cups

1¹/2 cups mayonnaise
¹/2 cup buttermilk
¹/2 cup finely shredded cheddar cheese
dash of Worcestershire sauce
dash of red wine vinegar
pinch of salt, black pepper and
*   red pepper*

Combine all ingredients and blend thoroughly. Store in tightly covered container. Use within 2 days.
　　　　　　　—Lisa Thomas

Beet Aspic

Must prepare ahead
Serves 8–10

"This is an unusual and colorful salad. It is a nice dish to serve with poultry."

1 (3-ounce) package lemon jello
1 (16-ounce) can diced beets
¹/2 teaspoon onion, grated
3 tablespoons sugar
2 tablespoons vinegar
³/4 cup water

Drain beets, while saving enough beet juice to make 1 cup of liquid. Add sugar and onion to beet juice and bring to a boil. Remove from heat and stir in jello and vinegar. Add ³/4 cup water and diced beets. Pour into an oiled mold and chill. Serve with sour cream.
　　　　　　　—Nan F. Bridgeman

Carrot-Raisin Salad with Honey Orange Dressing

Must prepare ahead
Serves 6

Dressing:
1 cup vegetable oil
1/3 cup honey
3 tablespoons frozen orange juice
concentrate, thawed
3 tablespoons lemon juice
1/2 teaspoon dry mustard
1/4 teaspoon celery salt
1/4 teaspoon paprika

Salad:
2 medium apples, diced
3 cups carrots, shredded
1/2 cup raisins

Blend all ingredients at high speed in blender or food processor, and mix until smooth. Cover and refrigerate at least 2 hours to blend flavors. Pour 2/3 cup of dressing into bowl and add apples, carrots and raisins. Toss until well coated. Refrigerate at least 2 hours. Toss with remaining dressing and serve.

—Kelley L. Wright

Marinated Vegetable Salad

Must prepare one day ahead
Serves 8

"So pretty, and so good! Every time I make this, everyone wants the recipe. I think it is served at every condolence meal at our church!"

1 (16-ounce) can tiny green peas, drained
1 (16-ounce) can shoepeg corn, drained
1 (16-ounce) can French-style green beans, drained
4 ounces pimento, diced, drained
4 stalks celery, chopped
1 green bell pepper, chopped
1 purple onion, chopped

Dressing:
1/2 cup vegetable oil
1 cup sugar
3/4 cup white vinegar
1 teaspoon salt
1 teaspoon pepper

Mix the vegetables together. Combine and bring dressing ingredients to a boil, then let cool. Pour over vegetables and refrigerate for at least 24 hours. Drain before serving. A jar of carrot salad makes a nice addition. Do not drain.

—Eva Ann McLean

Israeli Vegetable Salad

Serves 8

8 medium tomatoes, diced
1 long European cucumber or
    2 medium cucumbers, diced
2 medium red or green bell peppers, or
    fresh pimentos, diced
3 tablespoons fresh parsley, chopped
3 tablespoons fresh coriander (cilantro),
    chopped (optional)
3 tablespoons green onions, chopped
    (optional)
2 to 3 tablespoons extra-virgin olive oil
    or vegetable oil
2 to 3 teaspoons fresh lemon juice,
    strained
salt and freshly ground pepper

Mix the diced tomatoes, cucumber, peppers, parsley, coriander and green onions. Add the oil, lemon juice and salt and pepper to taste. Serve at room temperature.   —Janet Epstein

Pasta Salad

May prepare ahead
Serves 8

1 (16-ounce) box of shell or elbow pasta
1 cup sugar
2 tablespoons vegetable oil, 3 if using
    olive oil
3/4 cup white vinegar
2 (15-ounce) cans shoepeg corn
1 (15-ounce) can green peas, drained
1 large green bell pepper, chopped
1 cup celery, chopped
1 large jar pimentos
onion to taste (optional)
1 teaspoon pepper (optional)

Cook the pasta according to package directions, drain. Mix sugar, oil and vinegar in a medium saucepan. Bring to a boil. Remove from heat and let cool. Mix corn, peas, green pepper, celery, pimentos and onion in a large mixing bowl. Add pasta. Pour sugar, oil and vinegar mixture over this. Mix well. Add 1 teaspoon pepper if desired.   —Janet Long

Dry celery leaves in a paper bag. Then crumble fine and use as seasoning.

Watergate Salad

Must prepare ahead
Serves 12–15

2 (3-ounce) packages pistachio instant
    pudding
4 cups milk
1 small can crushed pineapple, drained
1 (10-ounce) bag miniature
    marshmallows
1 (8-ounce) container frozen whipped
    topping, thawed
1 small jar green cherries, drained and
    chopped

Mix pudding and milk in a large
bowl. Add pineapple, marshmallows
and half of the jar of cherries. Mix
well. Fold in whipped topping.
Garnish with remaining cherries.
Refrigerate for at least two hours
or overnight.   —Tracy Roberts

Apple and Orange Slaw

May prepare ahead
Low fat and low calorie
Serves 4

1¹/2 cups cabbage, finely shredded
1 (10¹/4-ounce) can mandarin oranges,
    drained
1 medium Red Delicious apple,
    cored and diced
¹/2 cup fat-free mayonnaise or fat-free
    whipped topping
1 tablespoon brown sugar or
    ¹/4 teaspoon sugar substitute

Place first three ingredients in a
bowl, tossing to combine. Combine
mayonnaise and brown sugar. Add
this mixture to the cabbage mixture
and coat well. Chill one hour.
—Holt A. Harris

Molded Slaw

May prepare ahead
Serves 10–12

"This recipe tastes better than
it sounds!"

2 cups cabbage, grated
¹/2 cup green bell pepper, finely chopped
¹/2 cup carrots, grated
¹/2 cup pecans
dash of salt and pepper
1 cup mayonnaise
1 (3-ounce) package lemon jello
¹/2 teaspoon vinegar
1 teaspoon grated onion (optional)

Dissolve jello in one half cup of
boiling water. Add other ingredients.
Stir and let stand in refrigerator. Put
in desired dish or jello mold before
it thickens.   —Leslie Wallace

*To improvise a ring mold, place
a greased tin can in the center
of a well-greased, 9-inch round
casserole dish.*

German Red Cabbage

Serve immediately
Serves 8–10

1/4 cup sugar
1/4 cup brown sugar, packed
1/2 cup apple cider vinegar
2 1/2 pounds red cabbage, shredded
2 slices bacon
1 Granny Smith apple, chopped
1/2 cup onion, chopped
1/4 cup water
2 tablespoons white wine vinegar
1/2 teaspoon salt
1/4 teaspoon pepper
1/4 teaspoon ground cloves

Combine first 3 ingredients, stirring until sugar dissolves. Pour over cabbage and toss to coat. Let stand 5 to 10 minutes. Cook bacon until crisp. Crumble and set aside. Cook apple and onion in bacon drippings, stirring until tender. Add cabbage mixture and water, bring to a boil. Cover, reduce heat, and simmer 10 minutes. Add vinegar and seasonings. Simmer uncovered 5 minutes. Spoon into bowl and sprinkle with bacon.

—Brownie Smyre

Oriental Salad

Serves 4–6

Salad:
1/2 head cabbage, finely sliced
1 (10-ounce) package of frozen green peas, thawed
1 package of Oriental flavored noodles, reserving the spice pack for the dressing
2 tablespoons sunflower seeds
2 tablespoons slivered almonds

Dressing:
1/2 cup vegetable oil
1/4 cup vinegar
spice pack from noodles

Sauté or bake sunflower seeds and almonds. In a large bowl, combine cabbage, green peas, crushed noodles, sunflower seeds and almonds. In a jar, mix oil, vinegar and spice pack. Shake well. Pour over salad and toss to coat. Possible additions: Cooked, cubed chicken, sliced grapes, or mandarin oranges.   —Laura Dixon

To keep fruit fresh looking, mix one package of instant French vanilla pudding, juice of one can of mandarin oranges, and 1/3 cup pineapple juice. Heat. The mixture will be stiff. Cool. Toss with fresh fruit.

Sweet and Sour Salad

May prepare ahead
Serve 6–8

Salad:

1 cup pecans
1 package Ramen noodles, uncooked and
 broken, discarding flavor packet
1 head of Romaine lettuce, broken into
 pieces
1 tomato, chopped
2 carrots, shredded
1 bunch broccoli, chopped
2 tablespoons butter

Dressing:

1 cup oil
1 cup sugar
1/2 cup wine vinegar
3 teaspoons soy sauce
salt and pepper to taste

Brown pecans and noodles in
butter in a skillet over medium
heat. Combine in a large bowl with
lettuce, tomato, carrots and broccoli.
Set aside. Combine oil, sugar, wine
vinegar, soy sauce, salt and pepper
in a blender. Blend well. Pour
over salad. —Christy Luce

Broccoli Salad

Must prepare 1 day ahead
Serves 8–10

Dressing:

1 medium purple or red onion,
 finely chopped
1 cup mayonnaise
1/2 cup sugar
3 tablespoons white vinegar

Salad:

1 pound cooked, crumbled bacon
1 cup pecans, chopped
1 cup raisins
2 large bunches of broccoli florets

Mix dressing together several
hours before serving or overnight
before tossing with salad. This
helps in cutting down the strongness
of the onion. When ready to serve,
put bacon, nuts and raisins in zip
lock bag and shake. This allows for
even distribution. Toss together salad
ingredients and add dressing.

—Britte Conner

To peel tomatoes, plunge in boiling water for 10 seconds. Skins will slip off.

Zucchini with Tomatoes and Dill

Serve immediately
Serves 6

3 tablespoons olive or vegetable oil
2 medium onions, finely chopped
1¹/₂ pounds ripe tomatoes, peeled, seeded
¹/₂ teaspoon sugar
salt and freshly ground pepper
1¹/₂ teaspoons paprika
¹/₃ cup fresh parsley, chopped
¹/₃ cup fresh dill, chopped
4 cups thickly sliced zucchini

Heat oil in a deep skillet or casserole.
Add onions and sauté over medium-
low heat about 7 minutes or until
just beginning to turn golden.
Add chopped tomatoes, sugar, salt,
pepper and 1 teaspoon paprika.
Reserve 1 tablespoon parsley and
1 tablespoon fresh dill for sprinkling,
and add rest of herbs to tomato
sauce. Cook, stirring often, over
medium-high heat for 7 minutes or
until thick. Add zucchini to tomato
sauce and sprinkle with salt and
remaining paprika. Cover and cook
over low heat, stirring occasionally,
for 30 minutes or until very tender.
If pan becomes dry, add a few
tablespoons water during cooking.
Serve warm, room temperature, or
cold, sprinkled with reserved herbs.
If you prefer bright-colored zucchini,
cook them for only 10 minutes.

—Janet Epstein

Bacon, Lettuce and Tomato Salad

Serve immediately
Serves 4–5

"This comes from my friend
Beth Cunningham."

¹/₄ pound bacon
4 slices firm, white bread cut into
*   ¹/₂-inch cubes*
5 tablespoons olive oil
¹/₂ head Romaine lettuce, cleaned and
*   torn into pieces*
1 tomato, sliced in thin wedges
1 tablespoon red wine vinegar
¹/₄ teaspoon salt
¹/₈ teaspoon pepper
4 thin slices or red onion
¹/₄ cup crumbled bleu cheese

Cook bacon until crisp and drain
on paper towels. Toss bread cubes
with 2 tablespoons oil. Cook bread
in frying pan over medium-high
heat, stirring often, until golden.
Crumble bacon. In a small jar, shake
together vinegar, salt and pepper,
until salt dissolves. Add remaining
3 tablespoons of oil and shake again
to combine. In a large bowl, toss
together lettuce, tomato, bacon,
onion, cheese and dressing. Top
with croutons.   —Beth Brittain

Tomato Soup Salad

Must prepare ahead
Serves 6–8

1 can tomato soup
2 (3-ounce) packages lemon jello
2 (3-ounce) packages cream cheese,
    softened
1 cup celery, chopped
1/2 cup onion, chopped
1 cucumber, peeled and grated (use coarse
    grater for the peeled cucumber)
1 cup mayonnaise
1/4 teaspoon salt

Dissolve jello in one cup hot water.
Heat soup. Blend mayonnaise and
cream cheese and beat into slightly
cooled soup. Add jello. Let cool and
add vegetables. Pour into desired
mold or dish and refrigerate until
congealed.   —Lindsay Lockett

Curried Chicken Salad

Needs to marinate one hour before serving
Yields 4–6 cups

Salad:
1 1/2 cups chicken breast,
    cooked and cubed
1/4 cup frozen peas, thawed
1/4 cup carrots, scraped and shredded
1 cup red cabbage, shredded
1/4 cup green apple, chopped
1/4 cup scallions, chopped
1/8 teaspoon celery seed
1 tablespoon golden raisins
1/4 cup celery, scraped and chopped

Dressing:
1 cup plain non-fat yogurt
1 tablespoon non-fat mayonnaise
3 teaspoons curry powder
3 tablespoons fresh lemon juice
freshly ground black pepper to taste
1 tablespoon Dijon mustard
2 tablespoons shallots, minced

Garnish:
4 large red cabbage leaves
4 cherry tomatoes
1 teaspoon fresh parsley, chopped

Combine the chicken, peas, carrots,
celery seed, raisins, shredded
cabbage, apple, scallions, and celery
in a salad bowl. Place all the dressing
ingredients in a small bowl and
whisk to blend. Pour the dressing
over the salad and toss well. Cover
and refrigerate for one hour. Place a
cabbage leaf, curved side down on
each salad plate. Mound salad into
the leaves and garnish with the
cherry tomatoes and parsley.

          —Heidi Latham

Japanese Chicken Salad

Serves 8

Salad:

3 or 4 cooked chicken breasts, cut into
    bite size pieces
1 head lettuce, torn; can mix spinach
    leaves and green leaf lettuce
3 green onions, sliced
1 (3-ounce) can chow mien noodles
1 (4-ounce) package sliced almonds

Dressing:

$^1/_4$ cup poppy seed, or less
4 tablespoons sugar
2 teaspoons salt
$^1/_2$ teaspoon pepper
4 tablespoons vinegar
$^1/_2$ cup salad oil

Mix the first three ingredients.
Just before serving, add noodles
and almonds. Combine dressing
ingredients in a bowl and whisk
until blended. Toss with the salad.

—Susan B. Allen

Chili Bean Salad

May prepare 1 day ahead
Serves 12–20

Salad:

1 (15-ounce) can kidney beans
1 (15-ounce) can lima beans
1 (15-ounce) can black beans
1 (15-ounce) can whole kernel corn
$^1/_2$ cup chopped green onions
$^1/_4$ cup chopped parsley and or cilantro
1 cup sliced celery and or zucchini
1 (4-ounce) jar diced green chilies,
    drained
$^1/_4$ cup chopped sweet red peppers and/or
    1 ($2^1/_4$-ounce) jar sliced black olives

Dressing:

2 tablespoons olive oil
$^1/_4$ cup white wine vinegar
1 teaspoon chili powder
$^1/_4$ teaspoon ground cumin
1 teaspoon dried oregano leaves or
    1 tablespoon fresh oregano, chopped
$^1/_2$ teaspoon pepper

Drain and rinse canned beans and
corn. Mix canned ingredients with
chopped fresh vegetables and herbs.
Add dressing of olive oil, vinegar,
chili powder, cumin, oregano and
pepper. Allow to marinate in
refrigerator for several hours or
overnight, stirring several times.

—Kay Moss

Girl Scout Taco Salad

Serve immediately
Serves 6–12

"This dish was made for our covered dish suppers at our Girl Scout meetings, led by sustainers Sandy Rankin, Billie May Carroll, Tuga Clements and Bev Bryant."

1 head of lettuce, cut in bite size pieces
1 to 2 tomatoes, diced
1 (15¹/2-ounce) can kidney beans, drained
1 (8-ounce) package taco-seasoned cheese
1 onion, diced (optional)
1 bag taco-flavored chips
1 bottle Catalina dressing

In a large bowl, toss together lettuce, tomatoes, kidney beans, cheese and onions. Just before serving, add one or two handfuls of crushed chips and dressing to taste. Mix well.

—Julie Heath

Pennsylvania Style Taco Salad

Serve immediately
Serves 5–7

Salad:
1 pound ground beef, browned, drained and rinsed under hot water
1 large head lettuce, shredded
1 medium onion, chopped
2 medium tomatoes, diced
8 ounces taco-flavored or cheddar cheese, shredded
1 (8-ounce) bag nacho or taco flavored chips, crushed

Dressing:
1 envelope Italian dressing mix
¹/2 cup sugar
2 tablespoons dry taco seasoning mix
3 tablespoons mild taco sauce

Combine ground beef, lettuce and onion in a large bowl. In a jar, mix Italian dressing according to package directions. Once dressing is mixed, add sugar, taco seasoning mix and taco sauce to dressing. Shake well. Pour dressing over salad and toss. Add cheese and crushed chips. Mix well.

Note: Dawn Brooks uses Catalina dressing to taste as a variation.

—Jill Hendrix

Vegetables

Raspberry Green Beans

May prepare ahead
Serves 8

"Delicious served hot or cold!"

2 pounds whole green beans, cooked
2 tablespoons sugar
1 cup vegetable oil
1 teaspoon salt
1 cup raspberry vinegar
1 teaspoon white pepper

If using fresh green beans, cook until tender (about 10 minutes), put in a casserole dish and set aside. If using canned green beans, drain well, put in casserole dish and set aside. Combine remaining ingredients and cook over low heat until sugar dissolves. Pour over green beans, cover and refrigerate at least 4 hours.

—Karen Minton

Deviled Eggs With Sun-Dried Tomatoes & Chives

Prepare ahead
Serves 10

6 large hard-boiled eggs, shelled
1/4 cup minced fresh chives
1/4 cup oil packed sun-dried tomatoes, finely chopped, drained
1 tablespoon olive oil
1 1/2 teaspoons minced thyme
Additional tomatoes, drained and cut into strips
1 teaspoon white wine vinegar

Cut eggs in half lengthwise. Scoop yolks into medium bowl. Mash yolks coarsely with fork. Finely chop 2 egg white halves; mix with yolks. Add tomatoes, chives, olive oil, thyme and vinegar. Mix well. Season with salt and pepper. Spoon about 1 tablespoon filling into each egg half, mounding slightly. Top with tomato strips. Make 8 hours ahead, cover and chill.

—Mary Ann Burgoon

Hard-boiled eggs will peel easily when cracked and placed in cold water immediately after taking out of the hot water.

Posh Squash

Serve immediately
Serves 8–10

2 pounds yellow squash, sliced
$1/2$ teaspoon salt
1 cup mayonnaise
$1/2$ teaspoon pepper
1 cup grated Parmesan cheese
$1/2$ cup soft bread crumbs
1 small onion, chopped
1 tablespoon of butter, melted
2 eggs, beaten

Cook squash in boiling salted water for 10 to 15 minutes in a covered pot. Drain squash and cool slightly. Combine mayonnaise, Parmesan cheese, onion, eggs, salt and pepper. Add cooled squash to mixture. Pour into $1^{1/2}$ quart greased casserole dish. Combine bread crumbs and butter and spoon over top of casserole. Bake at 350 degrees for 30 minutes.

—Robin Ward Hackney

Whenever fresh minced onion is needed in a recipe, use a cabbage grater. It also works great on hard-boiled eggs for egg salad or potato salad.

Spinach Stuffed Squash

Serves 6–8

4 yellow squash
melted butter
salt and pepper
Parmesan cheese

Spinach Stuffing:

2 (10-ounce) packages frozen chopped
    spinach, cooked and drained
$1/2$ cup chopped onion
2 tablespoons red wine vinegar
$1/2$ cup butter
1 cup sour cream
1 teaspoon salt
$1/4$ teaspoon pepper
bread crumbs
butter

Cook whole squash in boiling salted water for 10 minutes. Very carefully cut each one in half and scoop out seeds. Brush the shells with melted butter and sprinkle with salt, pepper and Parmesan cheese. Set aside. Sauté onions in butter until tender. Add spinach, salt, pepper, sour cream and vinegar; blend well. Stuff each squash shell with spinach mixture and sprinkle with additional Parmesan cheese and bread crumbs. Dot with butter and bake at 350 degrees for 15 minutes.

—Cathryn Beasley

Impossible Zucchini-Tomato Pie

Prepare ahead
Serves 6–8

2 cups zucchini, chopped
3/4 cup biscuit baking mix
1 cup tomato, chopped
3 eggs
1/2 cup onion, chopped
1/2 teaspoon salt
1/3 cup Parmesan cheese
1/4 teaspoon pepper
1 1/2 cups milk

Grease 10-inch pie plate. Sprinkle zucchini, tomato, onion and cheese in dish. Beat other ingredients until smooth. Pour over vegetables. Bake at 400 degrees about 30 minutes or until knife inserted in center comes out clean. Cool 5 minutes before serving.

—Lindsay Lockett

A good way to chop an onion with no tears is to place the cutting board on the stove and turn the vent fan on high.

Stuffed Tomatoes

Prepare ahead
Serves 10

1 (10-ounce) package frozen whole
    kernel corn
10 plum tomatoes
1 (16-ounce) can kidney beans, rinsed
    and drained
1 (4.5-ounce) can chopped green chilies
3 tablespoons vegetable oil
3 tablespoons apple cider vinegar
1/2 teaspoon dried oregano
1/4 teaspoon salt
2 tablespoons chopped cilantro or
    2 teaspoons ground coriander
1/4 teaspoon pepper
dash of sugar

Cook corn as directed on package. Cool. Cut tomatoes in half lengthwise; scoop out pulp to form shells. Place tomato shells outside down on paper towels to drain. Combine corn, beans and chilies in a bowl. Combine oil and next 6 ingredients in a jar. Cover tightly and shake vigorously. Pour over corn mixture, stirring gently to coat. Cover and chill. Spoon corn mixture into tomato shells. Serve cool.

—Laura Williams Newman

Eggplant and Tomato Casserole

May prepare ahead
Serves 6

1 eggplant (1¹/₄ pounds)
¹/₂ cup shortening
1 large onion, sliced
1 large green bell pepper, sliced
¹/₄ teaspoon ground black pepper
1¹/₂ teaspoons salt
¹/₂ teaspoon ground basil
4 large fresh tomatoes
¹/₂ cup grated sharp American cheese
¹/₂ cup soft bread crumbs

Peel eggplant and cut into crosswise slices about ¹/₄ inch thick. Sauté in 6 tablespoons of the shortening, adding the shortening as needed. Set aside. Sauté peppers and onions in the remaining shortening. Place in a 2 quart casserole alternating with layers of eggplant, beginning and ending with eggplant, sprinkling each layer with a mixture of seasonings. Slice tomatoes and arrange over the top. Combine bread crumbs with cheese and sprinkle over tomatoes. Bake in a preheated moderate oven at 350 degrees for 45 minutes or until browned on top. Can add sliced or diced leftover meats for a meal-in-one.

—Nancy Reid

Dip tomatoes and peaches in boiling water for 1 minute for easy peeling.

Zucchini Squash Casserole

Serves 8–10

"This recipe was shared with me by my sister-in law. It belongs to her mother, Mary Lou Johns and has become a family favorite!"

4 (6- to 8-inch) zucchini, cubed
4 (6- to 8-inch) yellow squash, cubed
1 medium to large onion, diced
1 teaspoon oregano
1 teaspoon black pepper
1 (12-ounce) carton cottage cheese
2 eggs
2 tablespoons mayonnaise
6 to 7 plum tomatoes, sliced
12 ounces shredded cheddar cheese
1 small bag seasoned stuffing mix
2 tablespoons Parmesan cheese

Sauté or steam zucchini, yellow squash, and onions until tender. Season vegetables with oregano and black pepper. Place squash mixture in a 9x13-inch baking dish. Whip cottage cheese. Stir in eggs and mayonnaise. Mix well. Pour cottage cheese mixture over squash mixture. Layer sliced tomatoes on top of cottage cheese mixture. Sprinkle shredded cheddar on top of tomatoes. Add seasoned stuffing mix to the top of the cheese. Sprinkle top of casserole with Parmesan cheese. Bake at 325 degrees for 45 minutes.

—Josie Conner

Island Yams

Serve cold or hot
Serves 6

"This simple, but exotic, recipe was conceived to feed hungry participants in the Schiele Museum's sea turtle conservation project. It is also great to feed to your husband just before suggesting that it is time to plan a trip to the Caribbean—for this purpose, be sure to add the mango and serve along with grouper."

1 (29-ounce) can sweet potatoes, in light syrup or 3 cooked sweet potatoes
1 (8¼-ounce) can crushed pineapple, in juice
¹/₂ cup fresh mango, chopped, optional
¹/₃ jar oriental sweet and sour sauce

Garnish:
¹/₄ cup cashews
¹/₂ cup dried banana chips
fresh mango, sliced, optional

Slice sweet potatoes. Add pineapple and mango, if desired. Toss with oriental sweet and sour sauce. This is great served cold for a beach picnic. May also be served hot. Just before serving, sprinkle liberally with banana chips and cashews.

—Kay Moss

Spinach Quesadillas

Serve immediately
Serves 4–5

Spinach Mixture:
¹/₂ tablespoon butter
10 ounces frozen chopped spinach, thawed and drained
¹/₄ pound fresh mushrooms, sliced
pinch nutmeg
pinch cayenne pepper

Quesadillas:
10 large flour tortillas
8 ounces cream cheese, softened
10 ounces Monterey Jack cheese, shredded
sour cream for garnish

Preheat oven to 375 degrees. Melt butter in large skillet and lightly sauté spinach and mushrooms. Stir in spices. Set aside. Drain if necessary. Place 5 tortillas on a cookie sheet. Top with cream cheese spinach mixture and Jack cheese. Place tortilla on top. Bake 7 minutes or until tortillas are crispy around the edges and cheese is melted. Cut into quarters. Serve hot with sour cream.

—Renee Long

Use an egg slicer to slice mushrooms and strawberries.

Julienne Vegetables

Serve immediately
Serves 10–12

3 medium zucchini
1 small red onion, peeled
3 medium yellow squash
1/4 cup white wine
3 large carrots, peeled
1/4 cup clarified butter
1 red bell pepper, seeded
1 teaspoon salt
1 green bell pepper, seeded
1/2 teaspoon white pepper
1/2 teaspoon chopped garlic

Cut vegetables into julienne slices
(1/8x1/8x2 inches). Mix together in
large bowl. In a skillet, heat clarified
butter to 175 to 200 degrees. Add
vegetables, salt, white pepper, and
chopped garlic. Stir and toss often for
2 to 3 minutes. Add white wine.
Make sure you do not cook the
vegetables too long. —Julia Burnett

Marinated Carrots

Prepare ahead
Serves 6–8

5 cups carrots, sliced thin
1 medium onion, sliced
1 medium green bell pepper, sliced
1 teaspoon Worcestershire sauce
1 teaspoon prepared mustard
1 teaspoon salt
1 cup sugar
1 teaspoon black pepper
3/4 cup vinegar
1/2 cup vegetable oil

Boil carrots in a small amount of
water until tender-crisp, about
5 minutes. Cool. Break the onion
into rings. Add the green pepper and
onion to the carrots in a 9³/4x9³/4-
inch baking dish. Make a marinade
with the remaining ingredients.
Stir well until the sugar and oil are
mixed. Pour over the carrot mixture
and marinate at least 6 hours or
overnight. Stir often. Spoon out
marinade when you are ready
to serve.   —Paula Stewart

*Anything that grows under the ground, start off in cold water—potatoes, beets,
carrots, etc. Anything that grows above the ground, start off in boiling water—
English peas, greens, beans, etc.*

Vegetarian Burritos

May prepare ahead
Freezes well
Low-Fat
Serves 8

"This is a great mix to freeze ahead of time. Also, since most ingredients can be found in your refrigerator and pantry, it's a fast meal. If time is restricted, drain the tomatoes as well and reduce cooking time to 30 minutes!"

2 tablespoons olive oil
1 large onion, diced
2 jalapeño peppers*, seeded, ribbed, and diced
4 garlic cloves, minced
2 (16-ounce) cans black beans, drained
2 (16-ounce) cans kidney beans, drained
1 (16-ounce) can whole kernel corn, drained
2 (16-ounce) cans diced tomatoes with juices
2 tablespoons ground cumin
3 limes

In a stock pot, add cold oil to warm pot and sauté onion, peppers and garlic until softened. Add 7 cans of ingredients and bring to a simmer. Add cumin and the juice of 3 limes. Stir well and simmer for 1 hour, stirring occasionally. Mixture will thicken. This flavorful filling replaces meat as your main course in this spicy burrito. Warm a burrito-size flour tortilla. In the center place ½ to ¾ cup of mixture and top with your favorite salsa, fresh tomatoes, lettuce, cilantro and nonfat shredded cheese, or nonfat sour cream. Roll and eat. *Use caution when handling jalapeño peppers. Look in the store for smooth skinned green jalapeños in the fresh vegetable section. The seeds and ribs are the spiciest. Remove for a mild flavor or dice the pepper whole for some zing. Wash hands immediately after handling peppers.   —Lindsay Meakin

Creamy Cauliflower

Serve immediately
Serves 6–8

1 head cauliflower, separated into florets
2 tablespoons butter, melted
1 envelope Sloppy Joe seasoning mix
2/3 cup sour cream
1/3 cup fine bread crumbs or dry stuffing mix
1/2 cup mayonnaise
1/4 cup milk

Steam cauliflower until tender, then spoon into shallow 1½ quart casserole. Measure 1 tablespoon Sloppy Joe seasoning out of packet, combine with bread crumbs and melted butter. Mix remaining seasoning with sour cream, mayonnaise and milk; spoon this mixture over cauliflower. Sprinkle bread crumb mixture on top, bake 25 minutes at 350 degrees.

—Ginger Hinman

Swiss Corn Bake

Serve immediately
Serves 4–6

1 (16-ounce) can whole kernel corn, drained
1 (5-ounce) can evaporated milk
3/4 cup shredded Swiss process cheese
2 eggs, beaten
2 tablespoons onion, finely chopped
pepper to taste
2 tablespoons melted margarine
1 cup soft bread crumbs
1/4 cup shredded Swiss process cheese

Combine corn, evaporated milk, 3/4 cup Swiss cheese, eggs, onion and pepper in bowl; mix well. Spoon into greased 1 quart baking dish. Sprinkle with mixture of bread crumbs and margarine; top with 1/4 cup Swiss cheese. Bake at 350 degrees for 25 to 30 minutes.   —Teresa Biggerstaff

Three Bean Bake

Prepare ahead
Serves 8–10

"The Best Baked Beans"

2 to 3 medium onions, chopped
1/4 cup bell pepper, chopped
1 (16-ounce) can pork and beans
1 (16-ounce) can kidney beans, drained
1 (10-ounce) can small lima beans, drained
1/2 cup ketchup
1/2 cup brown sugar, packed
1/2 teaspoon black pepper
2 tablespoons lemon juice or vinegar
dash of garlic powder
1/2 teaspoon salt
4 slices bacon, cooked

Sauté onions and pepper in bacon grease. Mix three different beans, ketchup, brown sugar, pepper, lemon juice, garlic powder and salt. Add to onion and pepper mixture and mix. Put mixture in large baking dish. Garnish with bacon strips. Bake at 350 degrees for 30 minutes, until bubbling.   —Ruth Everhart

A teaspoon of lemon juice or vinegar added to green vegetables will help them retain their color while cooking.

Festive Onions

Serve immediately
Serves 6

4 cups onions, sliced
5 tablespoons butter
2 eggs
1 cup cream, or undiluted canned milk
2/3 cup Parmesan cheese, grated
salt and pepper

Sauté the onions in the butter until they are transparent and then put them in a baking dish. Beat the eggs until they are light and mix in the cream and a dash of salt and pepper. Pour this mixture over the onions, sprinkle the Parmesan cheese on top and bake uncovered for 15 minutes in a 425 degree oven.

—Mrs. Plato Pearson, Jr.

Hashbrown Potatoes

Serves 8–10

2 pounds hash browns, frozen chunks
1 1/2 teaspoons garlic, minced
2 (10 3/4-ounce) cans cream of
  potato soup
8 ounces cheese, shredded
8 ounces sour cream

Place hashbrowns in a 9x13-inch pan. Let thaw. Mix all ingredients together, leaving enough cheese for the top of the casserole. Bake for 1 hour at 350 degrees.

—Rhonda McLean

Roasted Mustard Potatoes

Low Fat
Serves 4

light vegetable oil cooking spray
1 teaspoon chili powder
1/4 cup Dijon mustard
2 teaspoons paprika
16 baby red potatoes
1/8 teaspoon cayenne pepper
1 teaspoon ground cumin

Preheat oven to 400 degrees. Spray a roasting pan 3 times to coat with the vegetable oil. Put the mustard, paprika, cumin, chili powder, and cayenne pepper in a large bowl. Blend with a whisk. Prick the potatoes several times with the tines of a fork and add them to the bowl. Toss to coat the potatoes evenly. Pour the coated potatoes into the prepared roasting pan, leaving a little space between them. Bake for 45 minutes.

—Heidi Latham

To keep potatoes from sprouting before using them, put an apple in the bag with the potatoes.

Crispy Sliced Potatoes

Serve immediately
Serves 4

4 medium to large potatoes
3 tablespoons chopped parsley, or
    herb of your choice
salt to taste
2 tablespoons butter, melted
1/4 cup grated cheddar cheese
2 tablespoons Parmesan cheese

Preheat oven to 425 degrees. Scrub
and rinse potatoes. Cut potatoes into
thin slices, not cutting all the way
through. Place potatoes in a baking
dish and sprinkle them with butter,
salt and parsley or the herb of your
choice. Bake potatoes in oven for
approximately 45 minutes, then
remove from oven and sprinkle
with cheeses. Bake potatoes for
approximately 10 more minutes
until they look slightly browned.
Make sure cheeses are melted and
that potatoes are soft inside. Check
the potatoes with a fork.

—Kimberly B. Witherell

Garlic and Herb Potatoes

Serve immediately
Serves 6–8

2 large garlic cloves, crushed
3 pounds baking potatoes, peeled
    and cubed
1 tablespoon fresh rosemary leaves,
    plus 2 to 3 sprigs for garnish*
1 teaspoon salt
1/4 cup olive oil
1/4 teaspoon freshly ground pepper

Sauté garlic and rosemary in oil 1 to
2 minutes. Add potatoes, salt, and
pepper. Sauté for 5 minutes. Remove
garlic. Raise heat to medium high
and sauté 20 minutes longer, turning
often, until potatoes are brown and
crisp. Garnish with rosemary sprigs.
*Substitute 1 to 2 teaspoons dried
rosemary if fresh is unavailable.

—Debbie Stover

*To keep mashed potatoes hot, cover and
place in a skillet of hot water. To keep
fluffy, add a bit of baking powder.*

Old-Fashioned Potatoes Au Gratin

Serve immediately
Serves 6–8

6 medium potatoes
1/4 teaspoon pepper
1 stick butter
dash of paprika
3 tablespoons all-purpose flour
dash of nutmeg
1 teaspoon salt
2 cups of milk
1 1/2 to 2 cups grated sharp cheddar
   cheese

Slice potatoes and cook until barely tender. Place these in a 2 quart baking dish. Blend butter and flour over low heat in medium sauce pan. Add seasonings. Slowly add milk. This mixture will be thin. Add cheese 1/3 at a time (saving 1/2 cup). Stir constantly until smooth. Pour over potatoes. Top with remaining 1/2 cup cheese. Bake at 350 degrees for 30 minutes.   —Beth Harwell

When fresh asparagus is plentiful and inexpensive, stock up. Blanch, cool and store it covered with water in containers in the freezer. When thawed, it tastes just like fresh-picked.

Asparagus Casserole

Serve immediately
Serves 10–12

"Great for company."

1 (15-ounce) can long stem asparagus
   spears, drained, reserve liquid
1/4 cup butter
5 tablespoons all-purpose flour
salt and pepper to taste
1/2 cup milk
1/2 teaspoon Worcestershire sauce
4 eggs, boiled and sliced
1/4 pound sharp cheese, cut into chunks
1/2 cup almonds, sliced
1 cup buttery cracker crumbs, crushed
dash of cayenne pepper

Drain the asparagus and reserve the liquid. Set asparagus aside. Melt the butter and gradually blend in flour until smooth. Add salt and pepper to taste. Gradually add 3/4 cup asparagus liquid and 1/2 cup milk. Stir until thickened and smooth. Sauce should be thick, but may add milk or asparagus liquid if too thick. Add Worcestershire sauce and cayenne pepper. Layer the casserole in an 8x11-inch baking pan as follows: asparagus, egg slices, cheese, almonds, repeat. Spoon sauce over the layers. Sprinkle the cracker crumbs over the casserole. Bake at 350 degrees for 20 to 25 minutes.
     —Robin Hackney

Baked Corn in the Husk

Serve hot
Serves as many as you need

corn in the husks, as many ears as
you need

Place the ears of corn in the husks on a cookie sheet to prevent loose husks from burning. Bake one hour at 350 degrees or 45 minutes at 400 degrees. Turn halfway through cooking. If corn is exposed, wrap in aluminum foil. Once cooked, the silks come off very easily. To reheat, wrap in wet paper towels and heat in the microwave until hot to the touch.   —Julie Heath

Aunt Betty's Broccoli Puff

Prepare ahead
Serves 6

"My Aunt Betty is an excellent cook, and I remember the summers I spent with her and Broccoli Puff and fresh garden veggies."

1 cup bread crumbs
1 (10-ounce) package frozen broccoli cuts
1 can cream of mushroom soup
2 ounces sharp cheese, grated
  (approximately 1/2 cup)
1/4 cup sweet milk
1/2 cup mayonnaise
1 egg, beaten
1 tablespoon butter or margarine, melted

Cook broccoli according to package directions and drain. Place the broccoli cuts in a 1 1/2x6x10-inch baking dish, greased. Stir together soup and cheese. Gradually add milk, mayonnaise and beaten egg to soup mixture. Stir until well blended and pour over the broccoli. Cover the mixture with bread crumbs and pour the melted butter over the crumbs. Bake at 350 degrees until the bread crumbs are golden brown, about 30 to 45 minutes.   —Terri B. Nixon

Tomatoes with Spinach

Prepare ahead
Serves 12

12 tomato slices
2 boxes frozen chopped spinach, thawed
1 cup bread crumbs
6 spring onions, minced
6 eggs, beaten
3/4 cup butter, melted
1/2 cup Parmesan cheese
1 tablespoon Accent Seasoning
1/4 teaspoon garlic powder
1/2 teaspoon thyme
1 teaspoon black pepper
1 teaspoon salt
1/2 teaspoon red pepper

Salt and pepper tomato slices. In a mixing bowl, combine the chopped spinach and the remaining ingredients. Pile the spinach mix on top of each tomato slice. Bake at 325 degrees for 15 minutes.

—Bet Pearson

Polenta with Tomato-Mushroom Sauce

May prepare ahead
Serves 4–6

Sauce:

2 teaspoons olive oil
1 medium onion, chopped
1 large garlic clove, minced
1 teaspoon dried basil, crumbled
1/2 teaspoon dried oregano, crumbled
1/2 teaspoon salt
pinch of dried crushed red pepper
1/2 pound mushrooms, thinly sliced
1/2 cup dry white wine
1 (14.5- to 16-ounce) can whole peeled
    tomatoes, drained, juices reserved,
    chopped
3 tablespoons fresh parsley, chopped

Heat the oil in a heavy medium saucepan over medium heat. Add the onion and cook until tender, about 3 minutes, adding 1 or 2 tablespoons of water if the onion sticks. Add garlic, basil, oregano, salt and red pepper. Sauté for 1 minute. Increase heat to medium high and add mushrooms. Sauté for 2 minutes. Add 1/4 cup wine and cook until dry, stirring occasionally, about 3 minutes. Add the remaining 1/4 cup wine and tomatoes with their juices. Season with salt and pepper. Bring to a boil and reduce heat. Simmer until reduced to 2 1/4 cups, stirring occasionally, about 30 minutes. Add parsley. Can be made one day ahead. Cover tightly and chill.

Polenta:

1 cup yellow cornmeal
1 cup cold water
2 cups canned chicken broth
1 cup fresh or frozen corn kernels
8 tablespoons Parmesan, grated
3 teaspoons olive oil

Whisk cornmeal and water in a small bowl to blend. Bring the broth to a boil in a heavy medium saucepan over high heat. Add the entire cornmeal mixture at once and stir until the mixture boils and thickens. Reduce heat, add corn and simmer until very thick, stirring often to prevent sticking, about 15 minutes. Mix in 5 tablespoons Parmesan cheese. Spoon the polenta into an ungreased 9-inch round cake pan and smooth the top. Cool the polenta completely. Can be made one day ahead. Cover and refrigerate. Bring to room temperature. Preheat broiler. Turn out polenta onto work surface, tapping on the pan if necessary to release. Brush one teaspoon oil over polenta. Cut into six wedges. Place oil side down on a non-stick cookie sheet. Brush the top of the polenta with 2 teaspoons oil. Broil until golden, about 3 minutes. Meanwhile, bring the sauce to simmer. Divide the polenta among plates. Spoon sauce over polenta and sprinkle with the remaining 3 tablespoons cheese and serve.   —Mona Fulton

Pasta & Rice

Orzo Pasta Salad

Prepare ahead
Serves 6–8

"This pasta dish gets rave reviews every time I serve it."

2 tablespoons white wine vinegar
2 tablespoons lemon juice
1 teaspoon Dijon mustard
1/3 cup extra virgin olive oil
1/4 cup chopped fresh parsley
2 tablespoons chopped fresh basil
1 1/2 cups orzo, uncooked
1 (14-ounce) can artichoke hearts, drained and quartered.
2/3 cup Parmesan cheese (the fancy shredded type)
4 ounces prosciutto
4 green onions

Combine first 3 ingredients in a blender. Blend thoroughly. With blender still running, add oil in a slow, steady stream; process until blended. Stir in parsley and basil (be sure to only use fresh, not dried). Set dressing aside. Cook orzo according to package directions; drain and rinse with cold water. Slice prosciutto and green onions (including the green tops). Combine orzo, artichoke hearts, Parmesan cheese, prosciutto, green onions and dressing; toss gently. Cover and chill at least 8 hours; the flavors mellow and blend over time.   —Shelly Carter

Summer Pasta Salad

May prepare ahead
Serves 6–8

"I like to serve this salad at luncheons with bread and fruit."

4 garlic cloves, finely chopped
1 1/2 cups olive oil
1/2 cup red wine vinegar
1 tablespoon Dijon mustard
salt, pepper and basil to taste
1 pound tri-colored pasta
1 bunch broccoli florets
4 ounces sun-dried tomatoes (oil-packed)
2 red bell peppers, julienned
1 green bell pepper, julienned
2 medium zucchini, diced
8 ounces smoked gouda or mozzarella cheese, shredded
1 cup grated Parmesan cheese

Combine the first 7 ingredients in a small bowl. Whisk together and set aside. Cook pasta according to package directions; rinse in cold water and set aside. Blanch broccoli in boiling water for 3 minutes, drain and rinse with cold water. Drain sun-dried tomatoes, reserving oil. In a saucepan, saute the red and green bell peppers in the oil reserved from the tomatoes. Add zucchini. In a serving bowl, toss the pasta, broccoli, peppers, zucchini, cheeses, sun-dried tomatoes, and dressing. Mix well. If planning to serve at a later time, only mix in half of the dressing, adding the remaining just before serving.   —Josie Conner

Noodle Pudding

"Excellent for dinner with ham and a side vegetable, or as a brunch dish."

1 pound wide egg noodles, cooked
1/4 to 1/2 cup sugar
16 ounces low-fat cottage cheese
2 teaspoons vanilla extract
1 cup golden raisins (optional)
7 eggs, beaten
16 ounces sour cream
1/2 cup melted butter
bread crumbs
cinnamon
sugar

Mix first 8 ingredients. Put in a buttered casserole dish. Top with bread crumbs and sprinkle with cinnamon and sugar. Bake in a 350 degree oven for 45 minutes.

—Patti Hunter

Easiest Pasta

Serve immediately
Serves 3

1 (9-ounce) package fresh dairy
   linguine or fettucine
1 (6-ounce) jar marinated artichokes
   with liquid
1/2 to 3/4 cup fresh grated Parmesan
   cheese
olives, optional

Cook pasta according to directions. Cut up artichokes and reserve oil. Toss pasta with artichokes and oil and top with cheese and olives.

—Carol Hauer

Lemon and Garlic Pasta

Serve immediately
Serves 2–4

1/2 pound spaghetti
2 garlic cloves, minced
1/4 cup olive oil
2 tablespoons butter
1/4 cup chopped fresh parsley
1 teaspoon grated lemon zest
2 teaspoons lemon juice
1 teaspoon salt
1/4 teaspoon pepper

Cook pasta in boiling salted water until done. In small pan heat oil and butter. Add garlic and cook 1 minute. Toss pasta with olive oil and add parsley, lemon zest, lemon juice, salt and pepper. Serve immediately.   —Cathryn Beasley

Spinach Stuffed Pasta Shells

Freezes well
Serves 8–10

2 (9-ounce) packages frozen, chopped
    spinach, thawed and drained
2 tablespoons diced onion
1 (12-ounce) carton fat-free cottage
    cheese
2 eggs or 1/4 cup egg substitute
1 cup shredded low-fat mozarella cheese
1/2 cup grated Parmesan cheese
1/2 teaspoon garlic salt
1 box large pasta shells
1 (28-ounce) jar fat-free or reduced fat
    spaghetti sauce

Mix first seven ingredients in a large
bowl. Cook pasta shells as directed.
Pour a thin layer of spaghetti sauce
in the bottom of a 9x13 casserole
dish (or two smaller dishes). Stuff
each shell with spinach mixture and
place in dish. Pour remaining sauce
over shells. Cover with foil and bake
at 350 degrees for 30 minutes.
Remove foil and bake an additional
15 minutes.   —Josie Conner

Herbed Pasta with Goat Cheese

10 fresh basil leaves
1 tablespoon fresh oregano
1/2 teaspoon jalapeño pepper (optional)
4 garlic cloves, slightly crushed
1/2 cup extra virgin olive oil
1/4 cup balsamic vinegar
1 cup chopped cucumber
1/2 pound goat cheese
2 pounds plum tomatoes, cut in pieces
salt and pepper to taste
Tabasco sauce to taste
1 pound corkscrew pasta noodles, cooked
    and cooled

Put first 7 ingredients, plus half of
the goat cheese into a food processor
and puree. Add tomatoes and blend
just until chunky (don't blend until
mixture is smooth). Pour over cooked
noodles, crumble the remaining goat
cheese over the pasta and sauce.
Serve chilled.   —Patti Hunter

*Put a tablespoon of butter in the water when cooking rice, dried beans, or macaroni,
to keep it from boiling over. Always run cold water over it when done to get the
starch out. Reheat over hot water, if necessary.*

Knopfli (Tiny Dumplings)

Serve immediately
Serves 6

3 pints salted water
1 1/2 cups sifted all-purpose flour
1/2 teaspoon salt
1/2 cup milk
1 teaspoon melted butter
2 eggs, beaten until light and lemon
    colored
1/2 cup all-purpose flour

Heat water to boiling point. Mix
well 1 cup of the flour, salt and milk.
Add butter and eggs. Beat together
until it snaps, then gradually add
other 1/2 cup flour. Cut by teaspoonfuls into boiling water. Boil until
they float to top (about 3 to 5
minutes). Lift out with slotted spoon.
Brown in skillet with additional
butter or pour browned butter over
dumplings.   —Barbara Voher

Grandma Litchke's Flat Dumplings

Serves 6

2 cups all-purpose flour
1 1/4 teaspoons baking powder
3/4 teaspoon salt
3 tablespoons shortening or half butter
2/3 cup chicken broth

Sift dry ingredients together. Cut
in shortening. Add enough chicken
broth to make dough. Roll onto
floured board 1/8 inch thick and cut
in desired strips. Cook in kettle of
chicken broth 10 to 15 minutes or
until done.   —Vicky West Heinrich

Asparagus Risotto

Serves 2 for entrée or 6 for side dish

"This is a wonderful dish and worth the trouble!"

1 1/2 pounds fresh asparagus
1 tablespoon chicken-flavor instant bouillon
2 tablespoons margarine or butter
1 cup arborio rice (Italian short-grain rice)
2 tablespoons grated Parmesan cheese plus shaved Parmesan cheese for garnish

Hold base of each asparagus stalk firmly and bend the stalk; the end will break off at the spot where the stalk becomes too tough to eat. In 10-inch skillet over high heat, heat asparagus ends, chicken bouillon and 5 cups water to boiling. Reduce heat to medium-low; simmer, uncovered for 5 minutes. With slotted spoon remove asparagus ends from broth and discard. Meanwhile cut remaining asparagus crosswise into 1/2 inch pieces. In broth in skillet over high heat, place cut up asparagus and heat to boiling. Reduce heat to medium low and cook 3 to 5 minutes until asparagus pieces are tender-crisp. Remove asparagus to a bowl and broth to another bowl. Wipe skillet dry. In same skillet over medium heat, add margarine and stir arborio rice until coated. Add 1/2 cup reserved broth to rice, stirring frequently until broth is absorbed. Continue cooking, adding broth 1/2 cup at a time, and stirring after each addition until all broth is absorbed and rice is creamy and tender, about 20 minutes. You may not need to use all the broth. Stir in cooked asparagus and grated Parmesan cheese. Top with shaved Parmesan.   —Ginny Hall

Pasta Primavera

Serve immediately
Serves 8

1 (8-ounce) package linguine,
    broken in half
1 tablespoon olive oil
3 green onions, cut into 1-inch pieces
2 garlic cloves, minced
3/4 pound broccoli, broken into flowerets
1/2 pound fresh mushrooms, sliced
1 (10-ounce) package frozen English
    peas, thawed and drained
1 small tomato, chopped
1 small green bell pepper, chopped
1/2 cup olive oil
1/4 cup minced fresh parsley
1/4 cup grated Romano cheese
2 tablespoons vinegar
1/2 teaspoon salt
1/2 teaspoon dried whole oregano
1/2 teaspoon dried whole basil
1/2 teaspoon dried whole thyme
1/4 teaspoon pepper
1/8 teaspoon ground red pepper

Cook linguine according to
package directions. Drain and rinse
with cold water. Sprinkle with
1 tablespoon olive oil and set aside.
Sauté onions, mushrooms, green
peppers, and garlic in 2 tablespoons
olive oil until crispy tender, add
to linguine. Arrange broccoli in
steamer. Steam 6 to 8 minutes. Add
vegetables and remaining ingredients
to linguine; gently toss. You can add
a sauce, such as a spaghetti sauce, or
serve as is.   —Susan Allen

Pesto Sauce

Prepare ahead
Serves 4

3 tablespoons dried basil
1/4 cup water
1/2 cup fresh parsley
3 tablespoons olive oil
1 teaspoon salt
1/2 teaspoon fresh ground pepper
1/3 cup grated Parmesan cheese
1 teaspoon minced garlic

Combine basil with water in a 1-cup
microwaveable bowl. Cover with
plastic wrap; vent wrap. Microwave
on high 3 minutes or until water is
absorbed. Puree in blender with
parsley, olive oil, salt and pepper. Stir
in Parmesan cheese and garlic. Toss
with 1 pound cooked pasta.

                              —Kristy Case

*To clean aluminum pots when they
are stained dark, merely boil with a
little cream of tartar, vinegar, or
acid foods.*

Cajun Red Beans and Rice

Must prepare ahead
Serves 8–10

2 pounds of dry red kidney beans
6 smoked sausage links
2 cups chopped shallots
1/2 teaspoon black pepper
1/2 cup chopped bell pepper
1/8 teaspoon cayenne pepper
1 1/3 tablespoons minced garlic
1/8 teaspoon crushed red pepper
2 tablespoons parsley
2 bay leaves
1/2 teaspoon thyme
1/8 teaspoon basil
5 drops of liquid smoke
1 meaty hambone
1 tablespoon salt

Soak kidney beans overnight in large bowl of water. Rinse kidney beans. Bring to a boil in water to cover in large pot. Boil 5 minutes and then drain and rinse (this cooks the sugar off the beans). Cut sausage into 1/2 inch thick rounds and then quarter rounds and brown in skillet. Combine all ingredients in large pot, cover with water and cook on medium heat for 3 hours. Remove 1 1/2 cups of beans and mash them; return to pot and cook 1 1/2 hours, stirring occasionally. Remove hambone. Serve over steamed rice.

—Susan Massey

York Chester Rice Pilaf

Prepare ahead
Serves 6

"Simple and easy. Great with chicken or beef."

1 (6.09-ounce) box rice pilaf
1 1/2 cups water
1/4 cup orange juice
1 tablespoon butter or margarine
2 tablespoons sliced or slivered almonds
1 tablespoon chopped fresh parsley
orange zest (optional)

In medium saucepan, bring water and orange juice to a boil. Add butter. Stir in rice and spice packet. Cover and reduce heat to low. Simmer 20 to 25 minutes or until most water is absorbed. Add 1/2 almonds and pinch of parsley. Fluff rice. Garnish with additional almonds, parsley and orange zest. For use as stuffing: great with cornish game hens—add 1/4 cup mushrooms, 1/4 cup diced celery and one small onion at the time you fluff rice. Stuff game hens, pork chops or chicken.

—Deborah A. Rhyne

Braised Mushroom Rice

Serve immediately
Serves 6–8

1 cup uncooked rice
1 tablespoon butter
1/2 teaspoon thyme
1/4 teaspoon oregano
1/4 teaspoon pepper
1/4 tablespoon salt
2 (10 1/2-ounce) cans chicken broth
3 tablespoons butter
2 cups sliced mushrooms

Sauté rice in butter, stirring until lightly browned. Put in oven-proof 1 1/2-quart casserole dish. Add heated broth and all other ingredients except for mushrooms. Cover and bake at 350 degrees for 20 minutes. Meanwhile, sauté mushrooms quickly in hot butter until lightly browned. Sauté only a few at a time, so that they don't steam. When rice is done, taste, add any seasoning above to taste and toss rice with mushrooms.　　—Jennifer Lynch

Cheese Rice

Serve immediately
Serves 4

3 tablespoons butter
3/4 cup green onions, chopped
1 cup uncooked rice
2 cups water
1/4 pound sharp cheddar cheese, cubed
1/2 teaspoon salt
1/4 teaspoon pepper
1/8 teaspoon hot pepper sauce

Melt 2 tablespoons of butter in a medium saucepan. Add green onions and cook until wilted. Add remaining ingredients and bring to a boil. Cover, reduce heat and cook for 20 minutes. Stir occasionally to prevent sticking. Add remaining 1 tablespoon of butter and serve.
　　　　　　　—Mona Fulton

Fried Rice

Serve immediately
Serves 8

4 cups cooked rice, 1 day old
1/4 cup vegetable oil
3 sprigs chopped green onions
1/3 cup chopped water chestnuts
1/2 pound salad shrimp
1 stalk celery, chopped
2 crushed garlic cloves
1 medium red onion, chopped
1/4 cup soy sauce

Omelet:

3 eggs, beaten
green onions, chopped (optional)
1 tablespoon oil

Heat oil in saucepan until almost sizzling. Add garlic and onion. Add chestnuts and celery and cook for 2 minutes. Add rice. Mix well. Add soy sauce and green onions. Cook 2 minutes. Rinse and drain shrimp. Add shrimp to mixture. Mix well. Season with salt and pepper. Add more soy sauce if desired. For the omelet, heat oil in saucepan. Add eggs and green onions (optional). Cook until eggs are done. Cut into strips or cubes. Mix omelet with rice mixture.   —Janet Long

Mexican Rice and Cheese Casserole

Freezes well
Serves 8

"This was always one of my Dad's favorite recipes!"

4 cups cooked rice
2 (3 1/2-ounce) can chopped green chilies
6 ounces grated Monterey Jack cheese
1/2 cup grated cheddar cheese
1/8 teaspoon black pepper
2 cups sour cream

Combine cheese, sour cream, chilies and seasonings. Fold hot rice into cheese mixture. Place in buttered 6x10-inch casserole dish. Bake at 350 degrees for 45 minutes.

—Shelly Carter

For more delicious pasta recipes, please see our Seafood section.

Main Courses

Aunt Dianne's Marinated Roast Beef

Prepare ahead
Serves 6–8

"This is a favorite recipe of my mother's. It was shared with her by her sister, Dianne."

1 (3 to 5-pound) chuck roast
1 tablespoon sesame seeds
butter
1/2 cup strong coffee
1 tablespoon vinegar
1/2 cup soy sauce
1 large onion, chopped
1 tablespoon Worcestershire sauce

Thaw chuck roast. Brown sesame seeds in butter. Add coffee, vinegar, soy sauce, Worcestershire sauce, and chopped onion. Pour over thawed roast and let sit in refrigerator all day (or overnight). Turn every few hours. Grill about 45 minutes or until done.   —Janet McBryde Long

Moresaka Soufflé

Serve warm
Serves 6–8

2 pounds eggplant
1 pound ground beef
1 cup onion, chopped
2 tablespoons butter
1 1/2 teaspoons salt
1 tablespoon parsley
1/8 teaspoon nutmeg
1/2 cup tomato sauce
2 cups soft bread crumbs
6 eggs, separated
1/2 cup Monterey Jack cheese, grated

Pare and dice eggplant. Soak in a bowl of cold water for 30 minutes. Meanwhile, brown ground beef and onion in butter. Rinse the eggplant in a colander and drain well. Season the eggplant with salt and pepper. Add seasoned eggplant cubes to the ground beef mixture and brown lightly. Add parsley, nutmeg, tomato sauce, and 1/2 cup of water. Simmer until eggplant is soft. Remove from heat, and stir in 1 1/2 cups of the bread crumbs. Combine well-beaten egg yolks with the eggplant. Beat the egg whites until stiff. Fold in the beaten egg whites and blend. Pour into a 2 quart dish. Combine remaining bread crumbs with cheese and sprinkle over the top. Bake at 350 degrees for 45 minutes.

—Gerri Critikos

Sausage and Ham Jambalaya

Freezes well
May prepare ahead
Serves 8–10

2 tablespoons oil
1 cup onion, chopped
1 bell pepper, chopped
3 ribs celery, chopped
5 green onions
1 (10-ounce) can tomatoes, chopped
   (reserve liquid)
1 (10-ounce) can tomatoes and green
   chilies, diced (reserve liquid)
2 cups ham, diced
4 tablespoons tomato paste
1/4 cup parsley, minced
2 garlic cloves, minced
1 bay leaf
1 teaspoon thyme leaves
1 teaspoon basil
salt and pepper to taste
1/4 cup Worcestershire sauce
3 cups water
12 pork sausage patties
1 pound smoked sausage
2 cups rice, uncooked

Halve the pork sausage patties and cut the smoked sausage into 1 inch slices. In a large dutch oven, heat the oil. Add the onion and bell pepper and saute until tender. Add the celery, green onion, and tomatoes. Cook until soft. Add the ham and tomato paste and fry the mixture until it begins to brown. Add the parsley, garlic, seasonings, Worcestershire sauce, reserved tomato liquids, and 2 cups water. Cook this gravy for 1 hour. In a separate large skillet, fry the pork sausage and smoked sausage. Discard the grease. Add the sausages to the gravy mix in the dutch oven. Rinse out the skillet with 1 cup water and add to the gravy. Place the rice in the gravy mixture and cover tightly. When it starts to bubble, lower the heat and cook until the rice is done (about 15 to 20 minutes, but test the rice toward the end). Several times during the cooking, lift the mixture gently to keep it from sticking. If the water is gone before the rice is cooked, add a little more hot water to the gravy.   —Kenna Watts

Sprinkle salt in the pan before browning meat. This keeps it from sticking.

Apricot-Pecan Stuffed Pork Loin

Serves 10

1 1/2 cups dried apricots
1/2 cup pecans
1 garlic clove
1/2 teaspoon salt
1/4 teaspoon pepper
2 tablespoons dried thyme, divided
1/4 cup molasses, divided
1/4 cup peanut or vegetable oil, divided
1 (5-pound) boneless, rolled pork loin
     roast
1 cup bourbon
1 cup chicken broth
1 cup whipping cream
1/4 teaspoon salt

Process first 5 ingredients until coarsely chopped. Add 1 tablespoon thyme, 2 tablespoons molasses, and 2 tablespoons oil. Process until finely chopped. Make a lengthwise cut down the center of each pork loin piece, cutting to, but not through, the bottom. Starting from center cut, slize horizontal to each side, stopping 1/2 inch from the edge. Flatten to 1/2 inch thickness with a meat mallet or rolling pin. Spread apricot mixture, roll and tie each loin half. Place seam side down in a roasting pan. Brush with 2 tablespoons oil and sprinkle with 1 tablespoon thyme. Bring bourbon, chicken broth, and 2 tablespoons molasses to a boil. Remove from heat and ignite.

The bourbon must be burned off on the stove or the oven will be flamed! Pour over roast. Bake at 350 degrees for 1 to 1 1/2 hours. When done, remove roast from pan. Add whipping cream and salt to pan drippings. Cook over medium heat until thickened.   —Brownie Smyre

Apricot Glazed Ham

Quick to prepare
Serves 6

1 fully cooked center cut 1-inch
     thick ham slice (approximately
     1 1/2 pounds)

Sauce:
1/2 cup apricot preserves
2 tablespoons prepared mustard
1 tablespoon water
2 teaspoons lemon juice
1 teaspoon Worcestershire sauce
1/8 teaspoon ground cinnamon

Heat sauce ingredients until preserves melt. Pour over ham slice. Pierce ham with sharp fork several times. Marinate for several hours. Grill until heated thoroughly.

                    —Cherry Howe

Veal Piccata

Quick to prepare
Serves 4

"Great with Fetuccine Alfredo."

4 veal scallops
3 tablespoons all-purpose flour
1/4 teaspoon salt
1/4 teaspoon pepper
2 tablespoons olive oil
1 tablespoon butter
1/4 cup shallots or green onions, chopped
2 tablespoons capers
8 ounces mushrooms, sliced
1/4 cup chicken broth
2 tablespoons fresh lemon juice

Place veal between sheets of waxed paper. Pound until 1/4 inch thick. Peel off waxed paper. Combine flour, salt, and pepper in a shallow bowl. In a skillet, combine olive oil, and butter over high heat until melted. Dip veal lightly in flour, shaking off excess. Place in skillet and sauté quickly until browned on both sides. Remove from skillet and keep warm. Add onions, capers, and mushrooms to oil and cook briefly. Add chicken broth carefully to skillet. Using a wooden spoon, scrape up any browned bits clinging to the pan. When sauce boils, return veal to the pan and cook briefly. Stir lemon juice into sauce and serve immediately.

—Cherry Howe

Broiled Lamb Chops with Mint Pesto

Quick to prepare
Serves 4

"Serve with Cucumber Salad or Broccoli Salad. This dish needs something green for color."

1 bunch fresh mint, leaves finely chopped
2 tablespoons walnuts, very finely
  chopped
4 garlic cloves, minced
1/4 cup olive oil
4 loin lamb chops, 1 1/2 inches thick

Preheat broiler. To make mint pesto, combine the mint, walnuts, garlic, and olive oil in a small bowl and mix well. Brush one side of each lamb chop with a little mint pesto. Grill under the hot broiler for 4 to 5 minutes. Turn, brush with more pesto, and grill about 4 to 5 minutes. Grill longer for medium-rare chops. Serve immediately.

—Holt A. Harris

Spaghetti Pie

Freezes well
May prepare ahead
Serves 6

"My family loves this 'dressed up spaghetti'. It is a great way to use any leftover spaghetti noodles and sauce (or make it fresh). This dish travels well and I use it frequently when a dinner needs to be prepared and taken to friends or a family member. Serve with tossed salad, garlic bread sticks and dessert."

6 ounces spaghetti noodles, cooked and
   drained
2 tablespoons margarine
2 eggs, beaten
1/3 cup Parmesan cheese
1 pound ground beef
1/2 onion, chopped
1 (15-ounce) can diced tomatoes
1 (6-ounce) can tomato paste
oregano and garlic salt to taste
1 (8-ounce) carton cream-style cottage
   cheese
1/3 cup mozzarella cheese, grated

Mix noodles, margarine, eggs, and Parmesan cheese. Arrange in a deep dish pie plate. Bake at 350 degrees for 5 minutes. Cook and drain ground beef and onion. Stir in tomatoes, tomato paste, oregano, and garlic salt. Spread cottage cheese and mozzarella over pressed noodles. Top with beef mixture and mozzarella. Bake at 350 degrees for 20 minutes. Slice it like a pie to serve.

—Holt A. Harris

When preparing a pan of lasagna, place the cheese mixture in a large resealable plastic bag with one corner snipped off. Then squeeze the mixture out evenly onto the noodles. It is easy, and there is no mess or big clumps of cheese.

Roulade of Beef

Serves 4

1 large onion, finely chopped
4 (¹/₂-inch-thick) bottom round steaks
¹/₂ teaspoon rosemary
1 dill pickle
4 strips bacon
2 tablespoons shortening
¹/₂ cup all-purpose flour
2 tablespoons paprika
1 garlic clove, minced
¹/₄ teaspoon thyme
¹/₄ teaspoon marjoram
2 cups beef broth
1 can tomato pureé
1 cup red wine
salt and pepper

Pound steaks until ¹/₄ inch thick. Salt and pepper steaks on one side and sprinkle with rosemary and half of the chopped onion. Place one dill pickle slice on each steak along with a slice of bacon. Carefully roll-up each dressed steak and fasten with a toothpick. Sauté the rolled steaks in hot oil until golden brown. Remove browned steaks and place them in a casserole dish. Add the other half of the chopped onion to the skillet and sauté 5 minutes. Add flour, paprika, garlic, thyme and marjoram to sautéed onion. Add the broth, stirring constantly. Then add the tomato purée and bring to a boil. Cook until smooth and thickened, stirring constantly. Add the red wine. Pour the sauce over the rolled steaks and bake at 350 degrees for one hour.   —Suzy Massey

For extra juicy, extra nutritious hamburgers, add ¹/₄ cup evaporated milk per pound of meat before shaping.

Spaghetti Casserole

Prepare ahead
Freezes well
Serves 8

"This recipe is best if it is made and refrigerated the night before, but it can be made and cooked in the same day."

8 ounces spaghetti noodles
1 pound ground beef
1/2 cup green bell pepper, chopped
1 medium onion, chopped
1 can tomato soup
1 (15-ounce) can tomato sauce
2/3 cup water
1/2 teaspoon salt
1 1/2 teaspoons Italian seasoning
1 (8-ounce) can corn, drained
1/2 cup olives, sliced, black or green
2 cups cheddar cheese, shredded

Cook the spaghetti, drain, and set aside. Cook the beef, onion, and pepper. Drain. Add the remaining ingredients. Combine with the spaghetti. Pour into a lightly greased 9x13-inch baking dish. Cover and refrigerate several hours or overnight. Bake covered at 350 degrees for 45 minutes.   —Lindsay Lockett

Susan's Hamburger Casserole

Freezes well
May prepare ahead
Serves 8–10

1 to 1 1/2 pounds ground beef
1 teaspoon salt
1 teaspoon sugar
2 (8-ounce) cans tomato sauce
1 garlic clove, minced
1 cup sour cream
1 (8-ounce) package cream cheese, softened
1 large onion, chopped
8 ounces cheddar cheese, grated
8 ounces vermicelli

Cook the vermicelli according to the directions on the package. Rinse and drain. Mix the sour cream, cream cheese, and onion with a regular mixer or a hand mixer until creamy. Let stand while preparing the meat. Brown the ground beef. Add the salt and sugar. Drain any excess liquid. Add the tomato sauce and garlic to the ground beef. Simmer in the pan for 20 minutes. Spray a 9x11 inch casserole dish with non-stick cooking spray. Spread the cooked vermicelli on the bottom. Using a spatula, spread the cream cheese mixture over the pasta. Pour the meat sauce over the cheeses. Top with the grated cheese. Bake at 350 degrees for 30 minutes.   —Sherry Abernathy

Cajun Meat Loaf

Serves 8–10

"Spicy—Not your ordinary meat loaf."

Seasoning:

2 whole bay leaves
1 teaspoon cayenne pepper
1/2 teaspoon white pepper
1/2 teaspoon nutmeg
2 teaspoons salt
1 teaspoon black pepper
1/2 teaspoon cumin

Mix all of these ingredients together well.

Meat mixture:

4 tablespoons butter
1/2 cup celery, chopped
3/4 cup onion, chopped
1/2 cup green onion, chopped
1/2 cup green bell pepper, chopped
2 teaspoons garlic, minced
2 teaspoons hot pepper sauce
1 tablespoon Worcestershire sauce
1/2 cup evaporated milk
1/2 cup ketchup
1 1/2 pounds ground beef
1/2 pound ground pork
2 eggs, beaten
1 cup dry bread crumbs

Melt the butter. Add the onions, celery, green pepper, green onions, garlic, hot sauce, Worcestershire sauce and mixed seasonings. Sauté until the mixture starts to stick, about 6 minutes. While stirring, add the milk and ketchup. Cook about one minute longer. Remove from heat and allow mixture to cool at room temperature. Remove bay leaves. Combine the beef and the pork. Add the eggs, cooked vegetables, and bread crumbs. Mix well. In the center of a greased 9x13-inch baking dish, shape the mixture into a loaf 1 1/2 inches high by 6 inches wide by 12 inches long. Bake uncovered in a 350 degree oven for 25 minutes. Then turn oven to 400 degrees and bake 35 minutes longer.

—Mona Fulton

To seal in the juices in steak, rub sugar on both sides before grilling. You will not be able to taste the sugar.

Enchilada Casserole

Quick to prepare
May prepare ahead
Serves 8

2 pounds ground chuck
1 medium onion, chopped
2 (8-ounce) cans tomato sauce
1 (11-ounce) can Mexicorn, drained
1 (10-ounce) can enchilada sauce
1 teaspoon chili powder
1/2 teaspoon dried oregano
1/2 teaspoon pepper
1/4 teaspoon salt
1 (6 1/2-ounce) package corn tortillas,
    divided
2 cups (8-ounces) cheddar cheese,
    shredded, divided
green chile peppers to garnish

Cook beef and onion in a large skillet until the beef is browned, stirring until it crumbles; drain. Then stir tomato sauce and next 6 ingredients into the meat mixture. Bring to a boil. Reduce heat to medium and cook, uncovered, 5 minutes, stirring occasionally. Place half of the tortillas in the bottom of a greased 9x13 inch baking dish. Spoon half of the beef mixture over tortillas and sprinkle with one cup of cheese. Repeat layers with remaining tortillas and beef mixture. Bake at 375 degrees for 10 minutes. Sprinkle with the remaining cheese and bake 5 additional minutes or until the cheese melts. Garnish with green chile peppers, if desired.

—Lin Washburn

Flank Steak Sandwiches

May prepare ahead
Serves 8–10

"This was the late Diane Myers' recipe. I lent it out and thought I had lost it when a friend said I've had this for 10 years. It is such a wonderful sandwich to take to ball games."

1 cup ketchup
1 1/2 cups water
dash of garlic salt
2 tablespoons mustard
2 tablespoons Worcestershire sauce
3 tablespoons cooking oil
1 1/2 teaspoons salt
1/4 teaspoon pepper
1 tablespoon onion powder
2 flank steaks

Mix all of the above ingredients and place the steaks in ziploc bag. Pour the marinade over them and refrigerate overnight, turning several times. Cook on the grill for 5 minutes on each side or longer. Put on a cutting board and slice in strips.

Sandwich Spread:
4 ounces blue cheese
1 stick butter
1/2 garlic clove
2 tablespoons mustard
1/2 teaspoon salt
dash of pepper

Serve on buns with sliced onions.

—Virginia M. Hall

Dr. D's London Broil

Prepare ahead
Serves 4–6

6 tablespoons salad oil
3 tablespoons apple cider vinegar
3 teaspoons salt
2 teaspoons black pepper
3 teaspoons basil
2 teaspoons rosemary
3 garlic cloves, minced
2 medium onions, chopped
1¹/2 to 2¹/2 pounds flank steak

Combine oil, vinegar, and seasonings in a shallow Pyrex dish. Brush on both sides of steak and let marinate at least 90 minutes per side. It is best to marinate 1 to 2 days. Can be marinated in large freezer bags in meat keeper to save space. Broil 3 inches from heat 5 minutes per side, basting with marinade; or grill on hot grill 4 to 6 minutes per side until desired doneness. The chef suggests serving medium rare, sliced thin. When grilling, keep onions on top of the meat.

—Mrs. Darrell C. Current

Janet's Favorite Marinade

Prepare ahead
Yields 31/2 cups

"Excellent marinade for London Broil."

1¹/2 cups vegetable oil
1/2 cup Worcestershire sauce
3/4 cup soy sauce
2 teaspoons mustard
2¹/2 teaspoons salt
1 teaspoon pepper
1/2 cup wine vinegar
1¹/2 teaspoons parsley
1/3 cup lemon juice

Mix all ingredients. Marinate the meat in the mixture before cooking. May marinate overnight. Grill or cook meat as usual.

—Janet M. Long

Mushroom Sauce

Serves 8 over meat
Worth the effort!

*1/2 ounce dried mushrooms, porcini or
    morel work well*
2 tablespoons olive oil
*3 tablespoons shallots, minced or may
    substitute 2 1/2 tablespoons onion,
    minced and 1/2 tablespoon garlic,
    minced*
1/2 cup white wine
1 1/2 cups cream
2 teaspoons Dijon mustard
*1 tablespoon fresh parsley, minced
    (omit if fresh parsley is unavailable)*

Soak mushrooms in one cup of
boiling water about 30 minutes or
until softened, stirring occasionally.
Carefully remove mushrooms from
liquid leaving any sandy grit in the
soaking bowl. If necessary, cut the
mushrooms so that no pieces are
longer than one inch. Strain liquid
by lining a small funnel with a
paper towel. Pour the soaking liquid
through the funnel into a container.
The towel will trap the small grit
associated with dried mushrooms yet
absorbs very little of this flavorful
cooking liquid. Reserve liquid. In a
warm sauté pan, add the oil and
shallots. Sauté just until shallots are
softened. Add the mushrooms and
stir to mix. Add the wine and
reserved liquid. Cook this mixture
over high heat to reduce it by half.

Add the cream and reduce again by
half. Add the mustard and parsley,
stirring to combine. If needed, add
salt and freshly ground pepper to
taste. Keep warm until served.

—Lindsay Meakin

Marinade for Shish Kabobs

Must prepare ahead
Serves 6–8

3/4 cup vegetable oil
1/4 to 1/2 cup pale dry sherry
2 garlic cloves, chopped
1/4 bottle Worcestershire sauce
salt to taste
*about 36 to 48 steak cubes, 6 per shish
    kabob, can use round steak as
    marinade tenderizes meat*

Mix all ingredients with a wire
whisk. Cover steak cubes with
marinade. Cover the container and
put in the refrigerator overnight. Stir
occasionally the next day. Alternate
steak cubes on skewers with bell
pepper and onion cubes, quartered
tomatoes or cherry tomatoes.

—Nancy Garrett

Black Chicken Barbeque Sauce

Use immediately for grilling marinade.
Yields: sauce for one chicken

"This sauce gets its' name because the sugar caramelizes during cooking and turns the sauce dark."

1/4 cup butter or margarine
2 teaspoons salt
1/2 teaspoon pepper
1/2 teaspoon paprika
2 tablespoons sugar
1 teaspoon Worcestershire sauce
1 tablespoon lemon juice

Melt butter and mix all ingredients. Use sauce throughout the grilling time. Works better if skin is left on the chicken.   —Kenna Watts

Warren's BBQ Sauce

Prepare ahead
Yields: 1 1/2–2 cups

"Great on chicken or pork."

2 to 3 dashes of hot sauce, optional
1 cup ketchup
1/2 cup water, more or less, depending on
. thickness desired
1/4 cup apple cider vinegar
1 tablespoon Worcestershire sauce
1 tablespoon sugar
3/4 teaspoon celery salt
3/4 teaspoon salt
1 teaspoon black pepper

Mix all ingredients together in saucepan. Bring to a boil. Let simmer 15 minutes.

—Robin Hackney

Spicy Barbecue Sauce

Prepare ahead
Yields: 2^1/2 cups

^{1}/2 cup vegetable oil
^{3}/4 cup chopped onion
1 cup water
^{3}/4 cup ketchup
^{1}/3 cup lemon juice
3 tablespoons Worcestershire sauce
2 tablespoons prepared mustard
1 teaspoon salt
^{1}/2 teaspoon black pepper
2 tablespoons sugar

Cook onion in oil until tender, but not brown. Add remaining ingredients in order listed. Simmer 15 minutes.   —Paula Stewart

Grilled Chicken with Polynesian Salsa

Prepare ahead
Serves 10–15

"I like to serve this dish with a cheese soufflé and fresh steamed asparagus."

20 chicken breast fillets (halves skinned and boned)

Marinade:

2 cups olive oil
1 cup red wine vinegar
1 cup soy sauce
2 cups pineapple juice
1 (8^1/4-ounce) can crushed pineapple
1 tablespoon ground ginger

Salsa:

1 cup chopped pineapple, canned or fresh
^{1}/4 cup chopped red onion (or vidalia)
^{1}/2 cup chopped green or red bell peppers
1 (11-ounce) can mandarin oranges or clementine (drained)
^{1}/4 cup lime juice
^{1}/4 cup chopped cilantro (fresh is best)
sugar, salt and pepper to taste

Rinse and dry chicken breasts. Mix the marinade. Marinate chicken overnight and grill. Serve with salsa.
                —Gail Macomson

Chicken-Pineapple Kabobs

Prepare ahead
Serves 4–6

4 chicken breast halves, skinned and
  boned
1/2 cup vegetable oil
1/4 cup soy sauce
1/4 cup dry white wine
1 tablespoon sesame seeds
2 tablespoons lemon juice
1/2 teaspoon garlic powder
1/2 teaspoon ginger
8 mushrooms
3 small zucchini, cut into 1-inch pieces
8 or more pearl onions
3 tablespoons water
1 (8-ounce) can pineapple chunks,
  drained

Cut chicken into 1 inch pieces. Combine next 7 ingredients, mix well. Combine marinade and chicken in large glass container; cover and marinate at least 8 hours. Combine mushrooms, zucchini, red pepper, onions and water in microwave-safe bowl. Cover and microwave on high 3 to 4 minutes. Drain vegetables and put on grill skewers along with pineapple. Put chicken pieces on separate skewers to ensure thorough cooking. Grill on high for 8 to 10 minutes or until chicken is done, rotating so it will cook evenly. Remove chicken and vegetables from skewers and toss together on large platter to serve.   —Ginger Hinman

Chicken Marbella

Must prepare ahead
Serves 10–12

"This is a wonderful dish for a dinner party! I will have to admit that I was shocked to find out the ingredients. If you don't like prunes, don't let that scare you. This dish was served at the Silver Palate in New York."

4 chickens, 2¹/2 pounds each, quartered
1 head of garlic, peeled and finely puréed
¹/4 cup dried oregano
salt and pepper to taste
¹/2 cup red wine vinegar
¹/2 cup olive oil
1 cup pitted prunes
¹/2 cup Spanish green olives
¹/2 cup capers with a bit of juice
6 bay leaves
1 cup brown sugar, packed
1 cup white wine
¹/4 cup Italian parsley or fresh coriander (cilantro), finely chopped

In a large bowl combine chicken quarters, garlic, oregano, salt, pepper, red wine vinegar, olive oil, prunes, olives, capers and a bit of juice and bay leaves. Cover and marinate overnight. The next day, preheat the oven to 350 degrees. Arrange the chicken in a single layer in a shallow pan and spoon marinade over it evenly. Sprinkle with brown sugar and pour white wine over the chicken. Bake for 50 minutes to 1 hour basting frequently with juices from the pan.   —Julie Heath

Chicken and Wild Rice

Freezes well before baked
Serves 14–16

"Great for serving at a large buffet!"

1 (5-pound) chicken or 2 (2¹/2-pound) fryers
2 (6³/4-ounce) packages quick cooking wild and long grain rice mix (the kind with the seasoning packet)
1 pound hot sausage
2 medium onions, chopped
3 (10³/4-ounce) cans undiluted cream of mushroom soup
bread and butter crumbs

Stew chicken. Using chicken broth from stewed chicken, cook rice according to package directions. Fry sausage, drain. Sauté onions in sausage drippings. Add soup to onions and sausage. Divide soup-sausage mixture and put into 2 greased 9x13-inch casseroles. Top with cut up chicken. Put rice on top of chicken. Put dabs of butter and bread crumbs on top of rice. Cover with foil and bake at 350 degrees for 30 minutes or until bubbly.

—Brownie Smyre

Grilled Honey Chicken Breasts

Prepare ahead
Serves 6

1/2 cup honey
1/4 cup plus 2 tablespoons butter or margarine, melted
1/4 cup fresh lime juice
2 tablespoons Dijon mustard
1 tablespoon chopped fresh rosemary
2 garlic cloves, crushed
1/2 teaspoon dried savory
1/2 teaspoon salt
1/4 teaspoon pepper
6 skinned and boned chicken breast halves
vegetable cooking spray

Combine first 7 ingredients in a large shallow dish. Sprinkle salt and pepper over chicken: add chicken to marinade in dish, turning once. Cover and marinate in refrigerator 2 hours. Coat grill rack with cooking spray; place on grill over medium-hot coals (350 to 400 degrees). Remove chicken from marinade, discarding marinade. Place chicken on rack; grill covered for 5 minutes on each side or until done.

—Lin Washburn

Cheesy Chicken Enchiladas

May prepare ahead and refrigerate
Freezes well
Serves 6

2 cups diced cooked chicken
1 (10³/4-ounce) can cream of
   chicken soup
1 cup sour cream
1 (4-ounce) can chopped green chilies
¹/2 onion, minced
1 teaspoon chopped cilantro
salt and pepper to taste
2 (8-ounce) cans salsa verde (or
   15 ounces green creamed
   enchilada sauce)
2 cups grated sharp cheddar cheese
10 to 12 soft flour tortillas

Set 1 can salsa verde (or ¹/2 enchilada
sauce), grated cheese and tortillas
aside. Combine all other ingredients.
Spoon mixture into tortillas. Roll
tortillas, placing flap side down in a
greased 9x13-inch glass dish. Pour
remaining salsa verde (or sauce) over
every tortilla to moisten. Cover
with cheese. Bake 30 minutes at
350 degrees.   —Kristy Case

Old Fashioned Chicken Pot Pie

Prepare ahead
Freezes well
Serves 4–6

"This is my family's favorite dish!"

refrigerated pie crusts
4 to 6 chicken breasts
3 tablespoons margarine
¹/4 cup all-purpose flour
1¹/2 cups half-and-half
1¹/2 cups chicken broth
¹/2 teaspoon salt
¹/4 teaspoon pepper
optional: hard boiled egg for garnish

Cook chicken breasts, reserving
1¹/2 cups of broth. (Or you may use
canned broth.) Place 1 layer of pie
crust in a square 2 quart baking dish.
Shred chicken breasts on this layer.
Melt margarine, add flour and stir
to make a roux. Slowly add chicken
broth until this mixture is smooth.
Continue to stir as you add half-and-
half slowly. Let this mixture become
thick. Add salt and pepper. Pour this
mixture over chicken. Place layer
of crust over pie. Bake 30 to 35
minutes at 400 degrees. Garnish
with sliced boiled egg.
                    —Beth Harwell

Pour cooled broth from meat or poultry into a glass jar with a secure lid.
Refrigerate upside down. The fat will harden and remain in the jar when
you pour out the liquid to use in recipes.

King Ranch Chicken Casserole

May prepare ahead
Serves 10

"My best friend in the world, Gail Dowis, gave me this recipe. Young people love it. I have used it for several parties. The leftovers are delicious!"

1 chicken, cut up
1 large onion, chopped
salt and pepper to taste
1 bell pepper, chopped
2 teaspoons margarine
1 teaspoon chili powder
6 flour tortillas
1 (10³/4-ounce) can cream of chicken
    soup
1 (10³/4-ounce) can cream of mushroom
    soup
1 cup Monterey Jack cheese, grated
4 ounces mild green chilies, chopped
1 (14-ounce) can diced tomatoes

Cook chicken (I use 1 package breasts, 1 package boneless thighs) with salt, pepper, and some onion. Cool, debone, and shred into small pieces. Dip three of the tortillas in chicken broth and place in bottom of greased 9x13-inch casserole dish. Melt margarine in large skillet and slightly sauté onion and pepper. Add seasonings, soups, chilies and tomatoes. Heat and stir until fairly smooth. Layer chicken, soup mixture, another layer of dipped tortillas; spread cheese on top. Heat until bubbly and cheese melts. Keeps well in refrigerator.　—Eva Ann McLean

Chicken Casserole Supreme

Serves 6

"My neighbor, Shirley Setzer, brought this to our family when our son was born. A great dish for gift giving."

1 cup uncooked rice
2 cups cooked chicken
2 tablespoons chopped onion
²/3 cup mayonnaise
1 (8-ounce) can sliced water chestnuts
¹/2 cup slivered almonds
1 (10³/4-ounce) can cream of chicken
    soup
1 (10³/4-ounce) can cream of celery soup
¹/4 stick margarine, melted
1 cup corn flakes, crumbled
vegetable cooking spray

Cook rice according to directions. Mix all ingredients together thoroughly, except margarine and cornflakes, and put in 9x13-inch casserole dish sprayed with cooking spray. Melt ¹/4 stick margarine and mix with 1 cup crumbled corn flakes. Sprinkle on top of casserole. Bake at 350 degrees for 45 minutes.
　　　　　　　　　—Leslie Wallace

Chicken and Artichokes

Serve immediately
Serves 4– 6

"I like to serve it with rice and a salad, for a complete meal."

salt, pepper and paprika
3 pounds chicken pieces
6 tablespoons butter or margarine
1/4 pound fresh mushrooms, sliced
2 tablespoons all-purpose flour
3/4 to 1 cup chicken broth
3 tablespoons sherry
1 can artichoke hearts

Preheat oven to 375 degrees. Put salt, pepper, and paprika on chicken pieces and brown in 3 tablespoons of butter. Place in oblong glass dish. Slice mushrooms and simmer in same pan in which chicken was browned but add remaining butter. Simmer a few minutes. Sprinkle with flour. Add chicken broth and sherry. Cook about 5 minutes. Arrange artichoke hearts around chicken pieces and pour mushroom mixture over them. Cover and bake for 1 hour.   —Susan Stroud Current

Gourmet Chicken Pizza

Serve immediately
Serves 4

1 prepared pizza crust, large
1 tablespoon olive oil
1/4 cup mayonnaise
1/4 cup Dijon mustard
1 package sliced, smoked ham
2 chicken breasts, cooked and shredded
red onion, sliced in rings
green bell pepper, sliced in rings
roma tomatoes, sliced thin
Italian seasoning
shredded mozzarella

Preheat oven to 350 degrees. Brush crust with olive oil and bake 8 minutes or until lightly toasted. Combine mayonnaise and mustard. Spread small amount on crust then top with slices of ham. Spread remaining sauce over ham. Layer chicken, onion, peppers, and tomatoes. Sprinkle with Italian seasoning, then cheese. Bake 10 minutes or until cheese is bubbly.
                    —Cathryn Beasley

Creamed chicken or turkey dishes will freeze, except for those containing hard-cooked eggs.

Fiesta Chicken Pizza

Serve immediately
Serves 4– 6

$1/2$ tablespoon olive oil
1 pound chicken, cut into chunks
1 teaspoon minced garlic, fresh or dried
1 tablespoon basil, dried
1 purple onion, chopped
1 green bell pepper, chopped
1 red bell pepper, chopped
1 yellow bell pepper, chopped
2 (12-inch) pizza crusts
2 cups pizza sauce
2 cups shredded mozzarella cheese
2 cups shredded mild cheddar cheese

Heat olive oil in skillet, sauté chicken. Add garlic, basil and onion; cook until tender. Add peppers. Remove from pan and set aside. Put 1 cup of pizza sauce on each crust. Mix cheeses together. Divide and put on top of the sauce. Top with chicken and vegetable mixture. Bake at 450 degrees for 10 minutes. Serve hot.

—Tracy Roberts

South of the Border Chicken Kiev

Must prepare Ahead
Serves 6– 8

8 chicken breasts, halved, deboned
   and skinned
7 ounces green chilies, diced
4 ounces Monterey Jack cheese, cut into
   eight strips
3/4 cup finely ground dry bread crumbs
2/3 cup grated Parmesan cheese
2 tablespoons chili powder
3/4 teaspoon salt
3/4 teaspoon ground cumin
1/2 teaspoon pepper
6 tablespoons melted butter

Tomato Sauce:

32 ounces tomato sauce
1/2 teaspoon ground cumin
1/3 cup sliced green onion
salt and pepper to taste
hot pepper sauce to taste

Flatten chicken breasts between waxed paper. Place 2 tablespoons chilies and one strip of cheese on center of each chicken piece. Roll up and tuck ends under. Combine remaining ingredients, except butter, to make crumb mixture. Dip each stuffed breast into melted butter, then roll in crumb mixture. Place chicken rolls, seam side down in 9x13-inch baking dish. Cover and chill 4 hours or over night. Preheat oven to 400 degrees and bake covered for 20 minutes, then uncover and cook 20 more minutes until chicken is thoroughly cooked. To prepare tomato sauce, combine all ingredients in pan and heat well. Pour heated tomato sauce over chicken.   —Nan Kirlin

Save the plastic liner bags from empty cereal boxes. Next time you need to pound steak, chicken breasts, nuts or crackers, place them inside the bag for no mess!

Chicken Lasagna

Serves 8

1 (8-ounce) package medium egg
   noodles, cooked
$1/2$ cup margarine
$1/2$ cup all-purpose flour
1 teaspoon salt
$1/2$ teaspoon pepper
1 teaspoon basil
4 cups chicken broth
4 cups cooked chicken
1 (24-ounce) carton cottage cheese
1 large egg
2 cups shredded mozzarella
$3/4$ cup grated Parmesan cheese

Cook egg noodles and set aside.
Melt margarine in large saucepan
over medium heat; stir in flour and
next 3 ingredients. Cook, stirring
constantly for 1 to 2 minutes. Add
broth, stirring until smooth; bring to
a boil. Reduce heat and simmer 5 to
8 minutes or until thickened and
bubbly. Stir in chicken and remove
from heat. Combine cottage cheese
and egg, stirring well. Spoon
$1/3$ chicken mixture in the bottom of
a lightly greased 9x13-inch baking
dish. Top with $1/2$ of the noodles,
$1/2$ cottage cheese mixture and 1 cup
mozzarella. Repeat layers, ending
with chicken mixture. Sprinkle with
Parmesan. Bake at 350 degrees for
1 hour. (I use reduced-fat margarine

and mozzarella, fat-free cottage
cheese and chicken broth.)

—Betsy Forbes

Kathy's Creamed Chicken Macaroni Casserole

Serve immediately
Freezes well
Serves 6– 8

"A real child pleaser at my house!
To make a "meal in a dish," mix in
$1/2$ cup steamed, fresh broccoli!"

$1 1/2$ cups uncooked macaroni
3 tablespoons margarine, melted
1 heaping tablespoon all-purpose flour
1 (3-ounce) package light cream cheese
1 (4-ounce) jar pimento
1 teaspoon salt
$1/2$ teaspoon pepper
1 cup milk
1 cup reduced fat chicken broth
2 cups chicken, cooked and cubed

Cook macaroni according to package
directions; drain and set aside.
Combine margarine, flour, cream
cheese, pimento, salt and pepper
in a saucepan over low heat. Add
milk and broth gradually, stirring
constantly. Heat to boiling and cook
for 3 minutes. Add chicken and
macaroni and pour into $1 1/2$-quart
casserole dish. Bake at 350 degrees
for 25 to 30 minutes.

—Josie Conner

Chicken Asparagus Sandwiches

May prepare ahead
Freezes well
Serves 4

2 cups cooked, deboned, skinned and
  chopped chicken
$1/3$ cup mayonnaise (may use light or
  fat-free)
$1/2$ cup diced celery
salt and pepper to taste
8 slices white bread
1 (10-ounce) can asparagus
$1/2$ cup low-fat margarine
1 package Shake and Bake or similar
  chicken coating

Combine chicken, mayonnaise,
celery, salt and pepper. Spread on
4 slices of bread (do not cut off
crusts). Arrange asparagus on top of
filling. Top with other four slices.
Melt margarine and brush on both
sides. Coat sandwiches in coating and
brown quickly in margarine on both
sides. Wrap in foil and bake at 350
degrees for about 20 minutes. May
be prepared ahead and refrigerated.
—Cheri Davis

Chicken Sauerkraut

Serves 4

4 chicken breasts
1 can of drained kraut
4 small slices of Swiss cheese
1 (8-ounce) bottle of Thousand Island
  dressing

Place chicken breasts in a deep
casserole dish. Spread drained kraut
on chicken breasts. Place swiss cheese
on top of kraut and pour Thousand
Island dressing over top. Cover and
bake for $1^1/2$ hours at 325 degrees.
—Leslie Wallace

*For potluck suppers and picnics where casseroles must stay warm for several hours,
wrap it in newspaper immediately after baking.*

Spicy Peppercorn Chicken

Serve immediately
Serves 4

*4 large halved chicken breasts, skinless
    and boneless*
1 tablespoon crushed whole peppercorns
2 teaspoons butter
1/2 cup orange juice
1/2 cup whipping cream
1/2 teaspoon tarragon leaves

Pound chicken breasts until 1/4 inch in thickness. Sprinkle with peppercorns. Add butter and chicken to heated skillet. Turn chicken once, and cook until chicken is done. Remove chicken, keeping it warm. Turn heat to high and add orange juice to pan and whisk in the cream and tarragon. Bring to a boil, stirring sauce until thickened. (Sauce will be the right consistency when you have reduced what you have by 1/2 of the original volume.) Spoon the sauce over the chicken breasts.

—Kimberly B. Witherell

Ulla's Bleu Cheese-Lemon Chicken

May prepare ahead
Serves 6

1/4 cup all-purpose flour
1 teaspoon salt
1 teaspoon rosemary (prefer fresh)
1/4 teaspoon pepper
6 whole chicken breasts, cut in half
3 tablespoons butter
2/3 cup sour cream (may use non-fat)
1/2 cup crumbled bleu cheese
2 tablespoons fresh lemon juice
1 tablespoon sliced green onion
2 tablespoons grated lemon peel

Preheat oven to 350 degrees. Combine first four ingredients in shallow dish and dredge chicken in mixture. Melt butter in large skillet over medium high heat and add chicken. Cook chicken until golden brown turning once (approximately 5 minutes). Transfer chicken to baking dish. Combine sour cream and remaining ingredients in small bowl. (This step may be prepared ahead.) Spread mixture over chicken. Bake until topping is golden and chicken is well cooked, approximately 30 minutes.

—Susanne Memolo

Chicken Salad Pie

Freezes well
Serves 8

2 cups cooked diced chicken
1 green onion, chopped
1/2 cup chopped pecans
1 1/2 cups chopped celery
1/2 cup shredded sharp cheddar cheese
1 cup potato chips crumbled

Dressing:
1 1/2 cups mayonnaise
1 tablespoon lime juice
1/2 teaspoon salt
1/2 teaspoon pepper
1/2 teaspoon Accent

Mix together chicken, onion, pecans, celery and cheese. Mix all ingredients for dressing and mix with chicken mixture. Pour in greased pie plate and top with potato chips. Bake at 350 degrees for 25 minutes.

—Beth Stanforth

Cynthia's Chicken and Vegetable Stir Fry

Serves 8

"This delicious recipe was given to me by my friend Cynthia Stark Anderson and is a family favorite."

2 pounds boneless chicken breasts,
  skinned
1 teaspoon paprika
1/4 teaspoon salt
1/4 teaspoon pepper
1/8 teaspoon garlic powder
1 large onion, thinly sliced
1 1/2 large green bell peppers, cut into
  thin strips
1/2 cup diagonally sliced carrots
1/2 cup diagonally sliced celery
1 1/4 cups chicken broth, divided
2 tablespoons cornstarch
3 tablespoons soy sauce
2 large tomatoes, cut into wedges
4 cups hot cooked rice

Cut chicken into thin strips; sprinkle with paprika, salt, pepper and garlic powder. Coat large electric skillet with cooking spray; allow to heat to 325 degrees (medium) for 2 minutes. Add chicken and stir fry for 3 to 4 minutes or until lightly browned. Add onion, green pepper, carrots, celery and 1/2 cup chicken broth; cover and cook 1 1/2 minutes. Combine 3/4 cup chicken broth, cornstarch and soy sauce, stirring until well blended. Mix well. Add to skillet, continue to stir well. Add tomatoes; cook 2 to 3 minutes more or until sauce thickens. Serve over rice.   —Mrs. Phillip J. Nixon

Cheesy Chicken Breasts

Serves 4

"My neighbor, Leslie Wyatt, made this for me and my husband. Since then, I have used this recipe on numerous occasions and been asked for the recipe many times! It is a great recipe for supper club groups or entertaining friends and relatives."

*2 whole childen breasts, skinned and
    boned, or 8 to 12 chicken strips*
2 egg yolks
2 tablespoons water
1/2 cup all-purpose flour
dash of salt and black pepper
dash of paprika, optional
1/4 cup bread crumbs, may use Italian
3 tablespoons Parmesan cheese
2 tablespoons margarine

Cheese Sauce:
2 tablespoons margarine
2 tablespoons all-purpose flour
1 cup milk
1 teaspoon Worcestershire sauce
1 tablespoon Parmesan cheese
3/4 cup cheddar cheese, grated

Flatten chicken with your hand. Whisk the egg yolks and water in a small bowl. Combine the flour, salt, pepper, paprika, bread crumbs, and Parmesan cheese in a separate bowl. Dip the chicken in the egg yolks mixture followed by the dry mixture. Melt the margarine in a frying pan. Brown the chicken on both sides. Then put the chicken in a shallow baking dish. Bake 20 minutes at 350 degrees. While the chicken is baking, make the cheese sauce. Melt the margarine in a sauce pan. Stir in flour but do not let it cook too long, or it will burn. Add the milk and stir until the sauce thickens. Season with Worcestershire sauce. Add in the Parmesan and cheddar cheeses. Stir until the cheese melts. Pour the sauce over the chicken when the chicken is done.   —Janet Long

Italian salad dressing is a wonderful marinade for meat or chicken.

Crab and Tomato Pie

Serve immediately
Serves 6–8

"This recipe is a combination of my crab quiche and tomato pie."

1 deep dish pie crust
1 tablespoon Dijon mustard
3/4 cup mayonnaise, can use low-fat
1 beaten egg
1/2 cup chopped green onions
1/2 teaspoon salt
dash pepper
2 teaspoons Worcestershire sauce
2 small tomatoes
1/2 teaspoon basil
1/2 pound crab meat or 1 can lump crab
    meat, drained

Spread piecrust with dijon mustard and bake 5 minutes. Mix egg, mayonnaise, cheese, onions, salt, pepper, Worcestershire sauce and crab meat. Slice tomatoes, drain, and sprinkle with basil. Arrange half of the tomato slices on bottom of pie crust. Pour crab mixture over tomatoes. Arrange remaining tomato slices on top. Bake at 350 degree oven for 35 to 40 minutes.

—Mary Ann Patrick

Crab Cakes

Serve immediately
Serves 6

"Crab Cakes fit for a King and Queen."

1 pound crab meat
1 egg, well beaten
3 slices bread, crumbled
1 teaspoon prepared mustard
3 tablespoons mayonnaise
1/2 teaspoon salt
dash of pepper

Blend all ingredients, shape into cakes, dredge in flour and sauté in margarine or butter (can use olive oil if you prefer) until golden brown.

—Lin Washburn

For best results, freeze any kind of seafood in water. Store in the freezer for 3 months.

Patsy's Crab Cakes

May prepare ahead
8 cakes or 18 small appetizers

1 egg, well beaten
¹/2 cup Hellmann's lite mayonnaise
2 shakes red pepper
12 saltine crackers
2 tablespoons butter
2 cans lump crab meat, flaked

Mix first 4 ingredients together
and fold in crab meat. Cover and
chill 2 to 3 hours. Form into patties,
18 small or 8 large. Fry in butter
over medium heat 3¹/2 minutes or
until golden brown on each side.

—Price Thrower

Crab Meat Spaghetti

Quick to prepare
Freezes well
Serves 8–10

1 pound Velveeta processed cheese
2 sticks butter
1 small container half-and-half
1 (12-ounce) package thin spaghetti
12 ounces mushrooms, sliced
2 tablespoons chopped parsley
4 to 6 green onions, finely chopped
1 small container pimentos
1 pound crab meat
pepper to taste

Melt the processed cheese and 1 stick
of butter in a double boiler. Then
add the half-and-half. Cook the
spaghetti. It is better if you slightly
undercook the spaghetti by 1 or
2 minutes. Drain the spaghetti.
Melt 1 stick of butter and sauté the
mushrooms, chopped parsley and
green onions. Mix all ingredients
in a large pan (soup size). Add the
pimentos and pepper and stir in the
lump crab meat. Bake in a 9x13-inch
pan in a 350 degree oven for 35
minutes. This casserole can also be
divided into 2 smaller pans. Bake
one and freeze the other.

—Alexa Crenshaw

Lime Tarragon Grilled Salmon

Serve immediately
Serves 8

8 (6- to 7-ounce) salmon fillets
1¹/4 cups olive oil
¹/2 cup salad oil
1 cup fresh lime juice
¹/4 cup dried tarragon leaves

Combine oil, tarragon, olive oil and lime juice. Divide marinade. Marinate fish in marinade for 3 hours. Grill fish until done, basting with reserved marinade while grilling. Rule of Thumb: Cook fish 10 minutes per inch. This applies for whatever cooking method (grilling, baking, broiling, etc.) is used.

—Anne Mallonee

Shrimp Mosca

Serve immediately
Serves 6

2 pounds large shrimp, peeled and
    deveined
1¹/2 sticks butter
2 teaspoons rosemary, put in cheesecloth
    bag
¹/2 cup Worcestershire sauce
¹/2 teaspoon celery salt
1 teaspoon salt
¹/2 cup bread crumbs
1¹/2 teaspoons black pepper
¹/3 cup Parmesan cheese
1 teaspoon red pepper
1¹/2 teaspoons minced garlic
1 teaspoon thyme

Put all ingredients (except shrimp, bread crumbs and cheese) in saucepan and cook slowly on low fire for 5 minutes. Do not boil. Put raw shrimp in baking dish in one layer. Pour sauce over shrimp. Sprinkle bread crumbs and cheese over shrimp. Bake at 400 degrees for 15 to 18 minutes. Do not overcook. Serve with crusty bread to soak up juices.   —Denise Smith

To remove fish odor from hands, utensils and dish cloths, add one teaspoon of baking soda to a quart of water.

Quick Shrimp Curry

Low calorie
Serves 5

2 tablespoons vegetable oil
1 pound large shrimp, peeled and
    deveined
salt and white pepper to taste
1 small onion, minced
1 garlic clove, chopped
1 tablespoon chopped fresh gingerroot
(optional: 1 teaspoon jalapeño pepper,
    minced and seeded)
2^1/2 teaspoons good-quality
    curry powder
^{1}/4 cup chopped fresh cilantro
2 tablespoons unsweetened flaked
    coconut
2 tablespoons roasted peanuts and
    ^{2}/3 cup milk, processed in blender/food
    processor for 30 to 45 seconds

Heat vegetable oil in skillet, add
shrimp and cook, stirring over
medium-high heat for 1 minute.
Remove shrimp to a side dish. Season
with salt and pepper to taste. Add
onion, garlic, ginger and jalapeño, if
desired, to the skillet. Cook, stirring,
over low heat for 2 minutes. Stir in
curry powder and cook 1 to 2
minutes longer, or until fragrant.
Add the coconut-peanut-milk
mixture; bring to simmer and cook
for 2 minutes to thicken slightly.
Return shrimp to skillet and cook on
low heat until shrimp are cooked
through, but still tender, about

3 minutes, then stir in cilantro
and serve.   —Aimee M. Ness

Shrimp and Fish Creole

Serve immediately
Serves 4–6

^{1}/2 pound shrimp
2 tablespoons chopped parsley
1 pound cod or other flaky fish
2 teaspoons paprika
1^1/2 cups chopped onion
^{1}/8 teaspoon cayenne pepper
^{1}/2 cup chopped green bell pepper
^{1}/2 teaspoon sugar
2 garlic cloves, minced
1 bay leaf
1 tablespoon margarine
1 tablespoon cornstarch
1 can whole tomatoes, in quarters
1 cup uncooked rice
1 tablespoon water

Cook fish and shrimp until firm.
Drain and set aside. Sauté onions,
green peppers and garlic in
margarine until tender, 5 minutes.
Add tomatoes, parsley, paprika,
sugar, cayenne and bay leaf. Cover
and simmer 30 minutes. Add fish
and shrimp to sauce, cutting fish
into flakes, cook for 5 minutes.
Blend together cornstarch and water.
Add to creole and cook, stirring until
slightly thickened. Cook rice and
serve the creole on a bed of rice.
                    —Cathy Barrett

Shrimp Scampi

Serve immediately
Serves 6

2$\frac{1}{2}$ pounds large fresh shrimp, peeled
    and deveined
1 cup butter, melted
$\frac{1}{4}$ cup olive oil
1 tablespoon dried parsley
1 tablespoon lemon juice
$\frac{3}{4}$ teaspoon salt
$\frac{3}{4}$ teaspoon garlic powder
$\frac{3}{4}$ teaspoon basil
$\frac{1}{2}$ teaspoon oregano
hot cooked wild or white rice per
    instructions on package

Place shrimp in a single layer in a
10x15-inch jelly roll pan. Set aside.
Combine next 8 ingredients; pour
over shrimp. Bake at 450 degrees for
5 minutes, then broil 5 minutes or
until done. Serve over rice.

—Rhonda Booker

Shrimp Savoy

Serve immediately
Serves 2– 3

24 precooked, cleaned medium shrimp
6 tablespoons butter or margarine
2 garlic cloves, chopped fine
dash cooking sherry
2 tablespoons chopped chives
Parmesan cheese (fresh is best)

Prepare shrimp. Sauté garlic and
chives in butter until hot. Add
shrimp. Turn several times in sauce.
Add a good dash of cooking sherry.
Turn more and cover with sauce.
Sprinkle with grated Parmesan
cheese. Turn quickly. Serve over
fettucine noodles or rice. Accompany
with a green salad and French bread.

—Nancy Garrett

Barbecue Shrimp

Serve hot
Serves 2– 4

2 dozen large shrimp
   (approximately 1 pound)
Seasoning Mix
1 teaspoon Worcestershire sauce
1/4 pound plus 5 tablespoons butter
1 1/2 teaspoons minced garlic
1/2 cup shrimp/oyster sauce
1/4 cup beer, at room temperature

Seasoning Mix :

1 teaspoon cayenne pepper
1/2 teaspoon thyme
1 teaspoon black pepper
1/2 teaspoon rosemary
1/2 teaspoon salt
1/8 teaspoon oregano
1/2 teaspoon crushed red pepper

Rinse shrimp; peel, leave tails on.
In a large skillet over high heat add
seasoning mix, Worcestershire sauce,
1/4 pound butter and garlic. When
butter melts, add shrimp. Cook 2
minutes shaking pan. Add remaining
butter and shrimp sauce. Cook and
shake 2 minutes, add beer, cook and
shake 1 minute. Serve hot with
French bread.   —Alice Krawczyk

Summertime Fresh Shrimp and Tomato Pasta

May prepare ahead
Serves 4

1 pound shrimp
1 tablespoon butter
2 garlic cloves, pressed
6 green onions, finely chopped
1 cup fresh basil, finely chopped
4 ripe tomatoes, finely chopped
1 pound pasta
6 ounces feta cheese, crumbled

Peel and clean shrimp. Melt butter
in skillet over medium heat. Add
garlic to skillet. Add shrimp to
skillet and cook until done. Put
aside shrimp and mix all remaining
ingredients in bowl and let stand
for one hour at room temperature.
Cook pasta according to package
directions. Pour shrimp and feta
mixture over pasta and serve.

—Susanne Memolo

Lobster Newburg by Pauline

May prepare ahead
Serves 4

"This recipe is from my mother-in-law.

4 tablespoons butter or margarine
1/2 cup hot water
2 cups fresh or canned lobster or 2 cups
    other shellfish such as scallops,
    shrimp, crabmeat or a combination
    of any of these
3 tablespoons all-purpose flour
salt and pepper to taste
1 (13-ounce) can evaporated milk
    (may use skim evaporated milk)
1/4 cup sherry wine
1/4 teaspoon nutmeg

Use large iron skillet; put in butter and water, cut lobster into bite size pieces and add to skillet. Simmer for 3 minutes only. Sprinkle flour over meat and stir. Cook over low heat to avoid lumps, 2 to 3 minutes. Add seasonings and milk. Stir 5 minutes until mixture thickens. Add sherry and nutmeg. Serve over toast, sliced tomatoes or rice. (Tastes better the second time around.)

—Annemarie Couture

Flounder with Horseradish Sauce

Low fat, Low calorie
Serves 4

2 cups water
1 medium onion, sliced
1 carrot, sliced
2 sprigs parsley
1 bay leaf
1 teaspoon salt
1 1/2 pounds flounder fillets
1 tablespoon margarine
1 tablespoon all-purpose flour
2 tablespoons horseradish
1/4 teaspoon paprika

Bring water, onion, carrot, parsley, bay leaf and salt to a simmer in large skillet. Simmer 10 minutes. While liquid simmers, roll up flounder fillets and secure with toothpicks. Place rolled fillets in stock and simmer an additional 10 minutes until fish becomes opaque. Remove from stock with slotted spoon and keep warm while preparing sauce. Increase heat until stock boils. Reduce stock by half until it equals about 1 cup. In separate saucepan, melt margarine. Add flour and cook 1 minute. Slowly stir in fish stock until sauce thickens. Remove from heat. Add horseradish and spoon sauce over fish. Sprinkle with paprika.   —Karen Soderstrom

Grilled Swordfish Steaks

Serve immediately
Serves 4

2 tablespoons freshly grated lemon peel
2 or 3 garlic cloves, crushed
3 tablespoons fresh (or 2 teaspoons
    dry) basil
2 to 4 tablespoons olive oil
    (to make paste)
salt and pepper to taste
4 (1-inch-thick) swordfish steaks

Combine first 5 ingredients to make
paste; spoon on fish, flip to other
side, apply paste again, cover and
refrigerate one hour. Grill over
medium high flame until cooked
or until fish flakes easily.

—Nan Kirlin

Swordfish Madagascar

Serve immediately
Serves 2

3 tablespoons butter, melted
1/2 cup all-purpose flour
1 pound swordfish, two slices
1 garlic clove, chopped
4 tablespoons white wine
juice from one lemon
parsley to taste
1/2 teaspoon salt
1 tablespoon green peppercorn, crushed
paprika to taste

Preheat oven to 450 degrees. Lightly
flour two pieces of swordfish. Place
in skillet with melted butter and
brown on one side for two minutes.
Turn and add garlic to skillet.
When garlic turns light brown, add
white wine, lemon juice, parsley,
peppercorn, salt and sprinkle of
paprika. Bake in 450 degree oven
for 5 to 8 minutes.   —Robin Pauli

*Allow 1/3 pound fish fillets per serving. Allow 1/2 pound per serving if fish
is whole.*

Jambalaya

May prepare ahead
Serves 6– 8

"Don't let the list of ingredients intimidate you. Once you have all your veggies chopped, this dish is very easy to put together. It can be served as a main course, with a large leafy salad and crusty bread, or as a side dish with grilled chicken."

1 tablespoon olive oil
1/2 pound shrimp
1/2 pound spicy sausage, sliced
1 medium onion, chopped
2 to 3 teaspoons cajun seasoning mix
2 cups rice (not instant)
1 green bell pepper, chopped
1 cup tomatoes, chopped
2 stalks celery, chopped
2 tablespoons tomato paste
1 cup green onion, chopped
1/4 cup chopped fresh parsley
3 garlic cloves, finely chopped
4 cups chicken or fish stock
1 bay leaf
15 fresh oysters (optional)

Heat oil and sauté sausage until no longer pink. Reserve. To pan, add onion, green pepper, celery, green onions, garlic and 1 teaspoon of the cajun seasoning mix. Sauté until vegetables are soft. Return sausage to pan. Add shrimp and sauté until pink. Add oysters, if using, and cook until edges curl. In a separate pot, place stock and bring to a boil. Add rice, tomatoes, tomato paste, parsley, bay leaf and remaining cajun seasoning. Cover, reduce heat to low and cook until rice is done, about 25 to 30 minutes. Combine rice and shrimp mixture and cook, covered, for 10 minutes.   —Barbara Emerson

Baked Seafood Salad

Prepare ahead
Serves 6

"Make it, bake it, hot for supper!
Make it, don't bake it, serve on
lettuce for luncheon!"

1 cup chopped green bell pepper
1 cup lobster
1/2 cup chopped yellow onion
1 can chunk tuna
2 cups chopped celery
1 teaspoon Worcestershire sauce
2 cups real mayonnaise
1 teaspoon salt
2 cups crab meat
dash of hot pepper sauce
2 cups shrimp, drained
potato chips

Mix all ingredients except chips.
Refrigerate. Crush chips and put
on top. Bake at 350 degrees for 30
minutes or until hot throughout.

—Nancy Garrett

Orange Roughy Tarragon

Low-Fat, low calorie
Serves 1

1/2 pound orange roughy fillets
white wine
1 fresh lemon
1 teaspoon salt
1 teaspoon garlic powder
1 teaspoon white pepper
butter
tarragon

Set oven to 350 degrees. Place fish
fillets in baking dish with a little
white wine to cover bottom of dish.
Squeeze about 1/2 fresh lemon on fish.
Mix salt, garlic powder and white
pepper, sprinkle over fish. Place a few
slices of butter on top and sprinkle
with tarragon. Cover with foil and
bake about 35 minutes. Pour yourself
a glass of wine, and when the wine is
gone, the fish should be done.

—Mary Loughridge Sessoms

Spicy Seafood Linguine

Low fat
Serves 6

"This recipe can become quite spicy. Add jalepeño chilies to taste. This is a wonderful meal to serve guests. It is a favorite of my husband's."

5 tablespoons jalepeño chilies, seeds
   removed, chopped fine
1/2 cup minced onions
1/2 cup celery, chopped fine
2 tablespoons vegetable oil
4 tomatoes, peeled and chopped
1 bay leaf
1 tablespoon minced parsley
1 tablespoon sugar
salt and pepper to taste
1 pound peeled, deveined raw shrimp
1 pound raw bay scallops
1 pound linguine, cooked
grated Parmesan cheese

Sauté chilies, onion, and celery in oil until onions are soft. Add the tomatoes, bay leaf, parsley, sugar, salt and pepper. Cook until most of the liquid has evaporated and the sauce is quite thick. Reduce the heat, add the shrimp and scallops. Cover and simmer about 5 minutes, being careful not to overcook seafood. Serve over linguine (prepared per package instructions). Garnish with Parmesan cheese.　　　—Alice Krawczyk

Scalloped Oysters

Serve immediately
Serves 8

1 pint oysters, drained
1/2 cup cracker crumbs
1/2 teaspoon pepper
4 tablespoons butter
1/2 teaspoon salt
1/2 cup heavy cream
1 tablespoon Worcestershire sauce
1 tablespoon grated onion

Preheat oven to 350 degrees. Place half of the oysters in a well-greased 2-quart casserole dish. Top with half of remaining ingredients except cream. Repeat layers. Pour cream over all and bake

—Leila Smith King

Creamed Scallops with Pasta and Tarragon

Serve immediately
Serves 6

"This is a rich entrée—great for a small dinner party."

1 pound fresh scallops, rinsed, drained well, tough side muscle removed, cut in 1/4-inch cubes
2 tablespoons butter
2 tablespoons olive oil
1/4 cup French vermouth or good white wine
1 teaspoon lemon peel, minced
1 tablespoon lemon juice
1/2 cup heavy cream
2 tablespoons cream cheese, minced
1/4 cup fresh grated American asiago or Parmesan cheese
1 tablespoon fresh garlic, peeled and minced
1 teaspoon salt
12 to 14 ounces fresh fettuccine-style pasta
2 tablespoons fresh tarragon (chervil or parsley may be substituted)

In a large skillet over high heat, melt the butter and oil together. When light smoke begins to appear and the pan is very hot, gently slide in the scallops. Stir fry two minutes or until lightly brown (the scallops will finish cooking in the sauce). With a slotted spoon, remove and spread the scallops on a large plate, leaving as much liquid as possible in the skillet. Add the vermouth or white wine, lemon peel and lemon juice to the skillet and reduce the liquid by half to concentrate the flavors. This will happen in a minute or two, so do not leave the pan. Turn off the heat and whisk in the cream cheese. Set the sauce aside. Everything may be made ahead to this point and refrigerated. Just before serving, cook the pasta according to package directions and drain. Warm the sauce and only then add the scallops, cheese, garlic and salt. Finally, toss the sauce with the hot pasta, sprinkle with tarragon and serve. Dried tarragon may be used. Add the tarragon to the sauce before removing from heat to enhance the flavor.   —Lisa Hall

Slip your hand inside a waxed sandwich bag and you have a perfect mitt for greasing your baking pans and casserole dishes.

Sara's Wild Rice-Shrimp Casserole

Freezes well
May prepare ahead
Serves 8

2 (10³/4-ounce) cans mushroom soup
1/4 cup chopped green bell pepper
1/4 cup chopped onions
1/4 cup melted butter
2 tablespoons lemon juice
2 (6-ounce) boxes Uncle Ben's original
    wild rice mixture, cooked
1 teaspoon Worcestershire sauce
1 teaspoon dry mustard
1 teaspoon black pepper
1 cup grated cheddar cheese
2 to 3 pounds shrimp (frozen or fresh,
    cleaned)

Sauté green pepper and onions in butter. Add soup, lemon juice, cooked rice and other ingredients together. Pour into buttered casserole. I like to use lots of shrimp—men like it this way! Bake at 375 degrees for 35 minutes. Casserole can be made in the morning or night before and refrigerated until evening meal. Freezes nicely but takes a long time to thaw. Have room temperature before heating. Cook until bubbly.

—Sara Stowe

Classic Fish Marinade

1 cup margarine
1 garlic clove, minced
4 teaspoons all-purpose flour
2/3 cup water
1 tablespoon sugar
4 teaspoons salt
1/4 teaspoon pepper
6 tablespoons lemon juice
1/4 teaspoon Tabasco sauce
1/2 teaspoon dried thyme

Sauté garlic in hot margarine. Stir in flour until smooth. Add remaining ingredients. Cook until thickened. Cool. Marinade will thicken when cold in refrigerator. Set out before cooking on grill. Baste fish while grilling.

—Patti Hunter

Heat lemons well before using and there will be twice the quantity of juice.

Southern Temptations

German Chocolate Cream Cheese Brownies

1 package German chocolate baking squares
5 tablespoons butter, softened, divided
1/3 cup of cream cheese
1 cup sugar, divided
1 egg
1 teaspoon all-purpose flour
1/2 teaspoon vanilla extract
2 eggs
1/2 teaspoon baking powder
1/4 teaspoon salt
1/2 cup all-purpose flour
1/2 cup pecans, chopped
1 teaspoon vanilla extract
1/4 teaspoon almond extract

Melt German chocolate with 3 tablespoons butter. Set aside to cool. Cream the cream cheese with 2 tablespoons butter in a small mixing bowl. Add 1/4 cup sugar, 1 egg, 1 teaspoon flour and 1/2 teaspoon vanilla, mixing after each ingredient. Set aside. In a large mixing bowl, beat 2 eggs and 3/4 cup sugar until thick. Add baking powder and salt. Mix. Add chocolate mixture and beat slowly. Add flour, nuts, and extracts. Place 1/2 of chocolate mixture in bottom of greased baking dish. Add cheese mixture on top of chocolate mixture and then dot with remaining chocolate. Use a fork to swirl batter.

Bake at 350 degrees until barely done (about 30 minutes). Keep refrigerated. These are wonderful cold also!   —Melissa Anderson

Greek Wedding Cookies or Kourabiedes

Makes 5 dozen

1 pound sweet butter
1/2 cup confectioners' sugar
1 egg yolk
1/2 teaspoon almond extract
1 teaspoon vanilla extract
6 tablespoons toasted almonds, finely chopped
1 jigger whiskey
4 cups all-purpose flour, sifted
3 cups confectioners' sugar, sifted

Beat butter and sugar until creamy, about 15 minutes. Add egg yolk, flavors, and almonds. Mix until well blended. Remove from beater and gradually add sifted flour to make soft dough. Pinch off pieces and shape into various designs (crescent, round, etc.). Place on ungreased cookie sheet. Bake at 350 degrees for 20 minutes. Place on flat surface sprinkled with confectioners' sugar. Sprinkle confectioners' sugar over cookies. Let cool.   —Gerri Critikos

Pumpkin Cheesecake Bars

1 (16-ounce) box pound cake mix
2 tablespoons butter, melted
2 teaspoons pumpkin pie spice
1 (8-ounce) package cream cheese
1 pound can pumpkin
1 (14-ounce) can sweetened condensed
   milk
2 teaspoons pumpkin pie spice
3 eggs
1/2 teaspoon salt
1/2 cup pecans, chopped

Mix the cake mix, melted butter and pumpkin pie spice until crumbly. Press into a 10x15-inch jelly roll pan. Beat cream cheese until fluffy. Gradually add sweetened condensed milk, mixing thoroughly. Gradually add pumpkin, mixing well. Beat in eggs. Add pumpkin pie spice and salt. Pour over crust. Sprinkle 1/2 cup of chopped pecans over top of cream cheese mixture. Bake at 350 degrees for 30 to 35 minutes, until firm. Cool. Chill and cut into bars.

—Barbara Emerson

White Chocolate Chunk Cookies

Makes 1 1/2 dozen

1/2 cup margarine/butter, softened
1/2 cup shortening
3/4 cup sugar
1/2 cup brown sugar, packed
1 egg
1 3/4 cup all-purpose flour
1 teaspoon baking soda
1/2 teaspoon salt
2 teaspoons vanilla extract
10 ounces white chocolate chips or
   coarsely chopped white chocolate
1/2 cup macadamia nuts, coarsely
   chopped

Cream together butter and shortening. Gradually add sugars, beating well with electric mixer at medium speed. Add egg and beat well. Combine flour, baking soda and salt. Add to cream mixture. Mix well. Stir in vanilla, white chocolate and macadamia nuts. Drop dough by 2 tablespoons, 3 inches apart, onto a slightly greased cookie sheet. Bake at 350 degrees for 12 to 14 minutes.

—Rhonda McLean

After using a measuring cup for shortening, use it to measure sugar, too. Once the sugar is poured out, use a spatula to easily scoop out the remaining sugar and shortening at the same time.

Betty's Cookies

May prepare ahead
Freezes well
Yields 3–4 dozen

1 cup shortening
1 cup sugar
1 cup brown sugar, packed
2 eggs
2 cups all-purpose flour
1 teaspoon salt
1 teaspoon soda
1 teaspoon vanilla extract
1 1/2 cups oatmeal
1 cup toasted rice cereal
1 cup chocolate chips
1/3 cup pecans, chopped

Cream shortening, sugars, and eggs. Add and mix dry ingredients and vanilla. Add oatmeal, cereal, chocolate chips and pecans. Mix well. Roll into small balls. Place on pan. Bake at 350 degrees for 12 to 15 minutes.   —Ibby Page

When freezing cookies with a frosting, place them in the freezer unwrapped for about 2 hours. Then wrap without worrying about them sticking together.

Aunt Katherine's Peanut Butter Cookies

May prepare ahead
Freezes well
Makes 4 dozen

"These are the best peanut butter cookies you can imagine!"

1 cup butter
1 1/4 cups brown sugar, packed
1 cup sugar
2 eggs
1 cup chunky peanut butter
2 cups all-purpose flour, sifted
1/4 teaspoon salt
1/2 teaspoon baking soda
1 cup peanut butter chips
1 cup dry roasted peanuts

Cream butter and sugars thoroughly using a mixer. Mix the rest by hand. Beat eggs into mixture one at a time. Fold in peanut butter. Sift together all the remaining dry ingredients and gradually stir this into the the peanut butter mixture. Fold the peanut butter chips and peanuts into the batter. Drop the batter from a teaspoon onto a lightly greased cookie sheet. Space the cookies about 2 inches apart. Bake at 325 degrees for 15 minutes or until the cookies are light brown around the edges.
                    —Julie Fleming

Choco-Grahams

May prepare ahead
Makes approximately 3 dozen

"A hit every time I serve them, and so easy to make!"

1 sleeve graham crackers
6 ounces semi-sweet chocolate morsels
1 stick butter
1 stick margarine
1/2 cup sugar
1 teaspoon vanilla extract
1 1/2 cups chopped pecans

Line a cookie sheet with aluminum foil. Break graham crackers into singles and line the cookie sheet. Sprinkle the chocolate chips over the graham crackers (make sure there are some on each cracker). In a saucepan, melt butter and margarine. Add sugar and vanilla. Bring to a boil and cook for 2 minutes, stirring constantly. Remove from heat and stir in the chopped pecans. Spoon the entire mixture over the graham crackers, making sure each is completely covered. Bake at 350 degrees for 10 minutes. Remove and cool completely. Store in airtight container in the refrigerator.

Special Shortbread Cookies

May prepare ahead
Makes 2–3 dozen

1 3/4 cups all-purpose flour
1 teaspoon vanilla extract
1 cup sugar
1 egg, separated
1 cup butter or margarine
3/4 cup pecans or other nuts, chopped

Cream all of the above ingredients except the egg white and the nuts. Spread into jellyroll pan with wax paper or your fingers dipped in cold water. Brush the top of pressed dough with egg white and press nuts into that. Bake at 275 degrees for 40 minutes (1 hour is too long). Cut while still hot but let cool in pan before removing.

—Mrs. William N. Thrower, Jr.

In recipes for rolled cookies, mold the cookie dough into balls and flatten with the bottom of a glass that has been greased or dampened and dipped in sugar.

Gunilla's Cookies (from Sweden)

Freezes well
Makes 5 dozen

$1/3$ cup sugar
2 to $2^1/4$ cups all-purpose flour
1 stick plus 3 tablespoons butter, softened

Mix butter and sugar until creamy. Add flour. You will need to work dough with hands and knead. Form into long rope-like strips about $1/2$ inch in diameter. Flatten with your fingers. Make a deep groove down the center of the strip with your thumb, but don't break through the bottom.

Topping:

Jam of your choice
$1/2$ cup coconut
$1/4$ cup sugar
5 tablespoons butter, melted
$1/2$ cup oats

Fill the groove in the strip of dough with the jam of your choice. Sprinkle the top of the strip with the topping ingredients. Bake at 350 degrees for 12 to 15 minutes until slightly golden. Cut into 1 to $1^1/4$ inch diagonal sections while warm.

—Jill Hendrix

Ooey-Gooey Butter Bars

Freezes well
Makes 36 bars

1 package yellow cake mix
1 stick butter, melted
3 eggs
1 cup coconut
$1/2$ cup pecans or other nuts, chopped
8 ounces cream cheese, softened
1 pound box confectioners' sugar
$1^1/2$ teaspoons vanilla extract

Mix the cake mix, butter, and 1 egg. Press into a 9x13-inch pan. Add a layer of coconut and chopped nuts. Mix cream cheese, 2 eggs, confectioners' sugar, and vanilla. Spread over first mixture of coconut and nuts. Bake at 350 degrees for 35 minutes. Cool and cut into small bars. Can be refrigerated but not a necessity. You may need to grease the 9x13-inch pan with a little bit of butter. —Stephanie Denton

Use a pizza cutter to easily cut bar cookies.

Double Chocolate Fantasy Bars

Makes 36 Bars

1 (18-ounce) box chocolate cake mix
1/3 cup vegetable oil
1 egg
1 cup nuts, chopped
1 can sweetened condensed milk
dash of salt
1 teaspoon vanilla extract
6 ounces semisweet chocolate chips

Preheat oven to 350 degrees. In large mixing bowl, mix cake mix, oil, and egg on medium speed until crumbly. Add nuts. Reserve 1 1/2 cups crumb mixture and press remaining mixture firmly in bottom of a greased 9x13-inch baking pan. Combine remaining ingredients in a small saucepan. Cook and stir over medium heat until chips melt. Pour evenly over prepared crust. Top with reserved crumb mixture. Bake 25 to 30 minutes or until bubbly. Cool. Cut into bars. Store loosely covered at room temperature.

—Leslie Wallace

Kathy's Trifle

May prepare ahead
Serves 10–12

1 package devil's food cake with pudding in the mix
2 small packages instant chocolate pudding mix
5 Heath candy bars, crumbled
1 (12-ounce) container whipped topping
2/3 to 3/4 cups coffee liqueur

Prepare cake mix in 9x13-inch pan according to directions. Divide the cake into 3 parts. Crumble one part into a trifle dish and sprinkle with 1/3 of liqueur. Spread 1/3 of the pudding over the cake, then sprinkle with 1/3 of the crumbled candy bars. Repeat twice. You may want to reserve the layer of whipped topping until just before serving. Pipe on or spread the topping. Then top with the remaining crumbled candy bar. Can be done a day or two in advance.

—Kathy Plemmons

When a recipe calls for melted semisweet chocolate chips, it is cheaper to use semisweet baking chocolate squares in the same amount ounce-for-ounce. After the chocolate is melted, nobody knows what shape it was to begin with!

Sundrop Pound Cake

Serves 10–12

"Sundrop is a soft drink bottled in Gastonia, NC. Its citrus flavor gives this cake a unique taste."

2 sticks butter, softened
1/2 cup shortening
3 cups sugar
3 cups all-purpose flour
5 eggs
1 1/2 teaspoons vanilla extract
1 teaspoon lemon extract
6 ounces Sundrop or other citrus flavored
    soft drink

Sundrop Glaze:
2 cups confectioners' sugar
2 tablespoons butter, melted
2 ounces Sundrop or other citrus flavored
    soft drink

Preheat oven to 325 degrees. Grease and flour a bundt pan. Cream the butter and the shortening. Gradually add the sugar. Add the eggs, one at a time, beating well after each addition. Slowly add the flour. Beat until mixed. Add the vanilla and lemon extracts. With the mixer on low, slowly pour in the soft drink, beating just until mixed. Bake at 325 degrees for 1 hour and 15 minutes. Cool slightly in the pan before turning out to a serving plate. While the cake is cooling in the pan, mix the confectioners' sugar, melted butter, and soft drink. After the cake is on the serving plate, pour the glaze over the cake.

—Barbara Vaher

Orange Crush Pound Cake

1 cup vegetable shortening
1/2 stick butter
2 3/4 cups sugar
5 eggs
3 cups all-purpose flour
1 cup orange crush soda
1 teaspoon vanilla extract
1 teaspoon orange flavoring
1 envelope whipped topping mix

Cream shortening, butter, and sugar well. Add eggs one at a time. Alternate flour with orange crush soda and add to mixture. Add flavorings and whipped topping mix last. Pour into a greased and floured tube pan. Bake at 325 degrees for 1 hour and 15 minutes.

Cream Cheese Icing:
6 ounces cream cheese, softened
3/4 stick butter
1 teaspoon orange flavoring
1 box confectioners' sugar
1 teaspoon vanilla extract

Beat cream cheese and butter. Add confectioners' sugar, vanilla, and orange flavoring. If necessary, add 2 tablespoons cream.   —Amy Mayes

Coca-Cola Cake

2 cups all-purpose flour
1 teaspoon baking soda
2 cups sugar
1 cup Coca-Cola
1 cup butter
1 1/2 cups mini-marshmallows
3 tablespoons cocoa
1/2 cup buttermilk
2 eggs, well beaten
1 teaspoon vanilla extract

Preheat oven to 350 degrees. Grease and flour 9x13-inch glass baking dish. Sift flour, sugar and baking soda in mixing bowl. Heat butter, marshmallows, cocoa and Coca-Cola in a double boiler until boiling. Pour over flour mixture and mix well. Stir in buttermilk, eggs and vanilla; batter will be thin. Bake 30 minutes. Ice while hot.

Coca-Cola Frosting:
6 tablespoons cocoa
6 tablespoons Coca-Cola
1 cup butter
1 pound confectioners' sugar
1 cup pecans

Combine cocoa and Coca-Cola in saucepan. Bring to a boil. Add butter until melted. Pour over sugar in mixing bowl. Add nuts and blend well. Spread over hot cake. It will harden as it cools.

—Merryman Cleveland

Heath Bar Cake

1 box German chocolate cake mix (and ingredients listed on box)
1 small can sweetened condensed milk
1 small jar caramel topping
1 (12-ounce) container whipped topping
6 chocolate toffee bars, crumbled

Prepare the cake mix as directed. After the cake bakes, randomly poke holes in cake with the blunt end of a wooden spoon. Pour sweetened condensed milk over the cooked cake. Then pour the caramel topping over the cake. Spread the whipped topping and crumbled toffee bars on top. Store in the refrigerator.

—Vicki Jones

To keep marshmallows from turning hard, store them in the freezer. When thawed, they are like fresh.

Victoria Sandwich Cake

"This is from my mother, Sylvia Holmes. This simple cake is traditionally served in England for afternoon tea."

1¹/2 sticks butter, softened
3/4 cup sugar
3 eggs
1¹/2 cups self-rising flour
1/2 teaspoon baking powder
3 tablespoons milk
2 tablespoons confectioners' sugar
zest of half an orange if using orange
    butter cream filling

Spray two 9-inch cake pans with vegetable oil spray and dust lightly with flour. Preheat oven to 375 degrees. In the bowl of an electric mixer, beat together butter and sugar until fluffy. Add eggs one at a time until combined. Slowly beat in flour and baking powder until the mixture forms a batter. Add milk and stir. Batter will be thick. Divide batter evenly between the two cake pans. Bake at 375 degrees for 25 minutes. After baking, allow the cakes to cook in the pans for 5 minutes, then turn out onto a cooling rack and cool completely.

Traditional Filling:
6 ounces seedless raspberry jam
1 cup heavy whipping cream, whipped
Or you can use this variation of the
    Traditional Filling

Orange Butter Cream Filling:
1 stick butter, softened
3 cups confectioners' sugar, sifted
2 teaspoons orange juice
zest of one orange, if using this filling,
    add half of the zest to the cake batter

Once the cake is cooled, place one layer on a serving plate and spread evenly with filling. Top with the second cake layer and then dust* with confectioners' sugar. When using the traditional filling, ice the bottom layer with the jam and cover with the fresh whipped cream. Then top with the second cake layer and dust with confectioners' sugar. A nice alternative is the orange butter cream filling. Simply whip all four ingredients together and spread the entire mixture on top of the first layer, then cover with the second layer and dust with confectioners' sugar. Because this sandwich cake is not frosted on the sides and top, it will not be "too filling" at four in the afternoon. It also looks beautiful if ringed with fresh berries at the base of the cake. Place cake in a covered container to store. If the traditional filling is used, the cake must be stored in the refrigerator. * To dust: spoon confectioners' sugar into a small seive. Hold the seive about four inches above the cake surface, lightly tapping the seive with your hand to send a dusting of powder over the cake.   —Lindsay Meakin

Streusel Cake

1 cup sugar
1/2 cup brown sugar, packed
1/2 cup shortening
1 egg
1 cup milk
1 teaspoon vanilla extract
2 cups raw apple, chopped and peeled
2 cups all-purpose flour
1 teaspoon baking soda
1 teaspoon baking powder
1/2 teaspoon salt

Topping:
3 tablespoons brown sugar
1 tablespoon sugar
1/2 cup nuts, chopped
1/2 cup coconut

Cream shortening, brown and white sugars together; add the egg. Add the dry ingredients alternately with the milk. Add the vanilla and fold in the apples. Pour into a greased 9x13-inch pan. Prepare the topping by mixing together the brown sugar, white sugar, and the nuts. Sprinkle over the dough, and then top with the coconut. Bake at 350 degrees for 40 to 45 minutes. Serve as is or top with whipped cream.

—Vicky W. Heinrich

If you get some egg yolk in egg whites to be beaten, just touch the yolk with a piece of bread. The yolk will adhere to the bread.

Triple Layer Chocolate Cheesecake

Serves 16

"Absolute favorite to everyone who tries this recipe. My friends refer to it as 'tri-color'".

1 (8.5-ounce) package chocolate wafer cookies, crushed (about 2 cups)
3/4 cup sugar, divided
1/4 cup plus 1 tablespoon butter, melted
2 (8-ounce) packages cream cheese, softened and divided
3 eggs, divided
1 teaspoon vanilla extract, divided
2 (1-ounce) squares semisweet chocolate, melted
1 1/3 cups sour cream, divided
1/3 cup dark brown sugar, packed
1 tablespoon all-purpose flour
1/4 cup pecans, chopped
5 ounces cream cheese, softened
1/4 teaspoon almond extract

Combine cookie crumbs, 1/4 cup sugar and butter in a medium bowl and blend well. Press into the bottom and 2 inches up the sides of a 9-inch springform pan. Combine one 8-ounce package cream cheese and 1/4 cup sugar. Beat until fluffy. Add 1 egg and 1/4 teaspoon vanilla and blend well. Stir in melted chocolate and 1/3 cup sour cream. Spoon over the chocolate crust. Combine remaining 8 ounce package of cream cheese, brown sugar and flour. Beat until the mixture is fluffy. Add 1 egg and 1/2 teaspoon vanilla and blend well. Stir in pecans and spoon gently over the chocolate layer. Combine 5 ounces cream cheese and the remaining 1/4 cup sugar. Beat until fluffy. Add the egg and blend well. Stir in the remaining 1 cup of sour cream, 1/4 teaspoon vanilla and almond extract. Spoon over the second layer. Bake 1 hour at 325 degrees. Turn off the oven and leave for 30 minutes. Open the oven door and leave another 30 minutes. Chill 8 hours and remove from pan.

Chocolate Glaze:
6 (1-ounce) squares semisweet chocolate
1/4 cup butter
3/4 cup confectioners' sugar, sifted
2 tablespoons water
1 teaspoon vanilla extract

Combine chocolate and butter in the top of a double boiler. Cook until melted. Remove from heat and stir in the remaining ingredients. Stir until smooth. Spread over the cheesecake while the glaze is warm.

—Cheryl Black

Chocolate Chip Cake

May prepare ahead
Serves 12–16

1 package yellow cake mix
1 small package instant vanilla
    pudding
3/4 cup oil
3/4 cup water
4 eggs
1 (6-ounce) package chocolate chips
4 ounces German chocolate, grated

Icing:
1 cup confectioners' sugar, sifted
1/4 cup milk

Mix all ingredients, except the two chocolates for 5 minutes. Fold in the chocolates. Bake at 350 degrees for 50 to 60 minutes. Cool in the pan for 30 minutes. While the cake is still warm, spoon on the icing. May put some grated chocolate on top.

—Tammy L. Sasser

To get a cake out of the pan, place a damp dish cloth on the bottom of the upside-down pan. Pat lightly.

White Chocolate Cheesecake

"This is the best cheesecake I have ever tasted. It is wonderfully light and not too rich. To speed preparation time, use the low setting on the microwave instead of a double boiler to melt ingredients but be careful not to over heat."

Crust:
1 box shortbread cookies, crushed
1/3 cup margarine, melted
1/3 cup ground walnuts or pecans
1/2 teaspoon ground cinnamon

Combine the above ingredients and press into the bottom of a 10-inch springform pan. Hold back 6 to 8 cookies from the box to keep the crust from being too thick. Add additional margarine to the crust when mixing, if necessary for binding. Bake at 350 degrees for 7 to 10 minutes, or until golden brown. Do not burn. Let cool.

Filling:
6 ounces white chocolate, finely chopped
3/4 cup heavy whipping cream
2 (8-ounce) packages cream cheese at
*   room temperature*
3/4 cup plus 2 tablespoons sugar
4 eggs
1 teaspoon vanilla extract

Combine the chocolate and 1/2 cup of the whipping cream in a double boiler. Leave until melted, stirring often. Cool to room temperature and whisk until smooth. Beat the cream cheese with the remaining cream until smooth. Gradually beat in sugar. Beat in eggs one at a time. Beat until smooth. Gradually add the cooled chocolate and the vanilla. Stir until well blended. Pour onto the cooled crust. Bake at 350 degrees on the middle rack in the oven for about 65 minutes, or until the center is barely firm and the top begins to crack. Cool 15 minutes. Increase oven temperature to 425 degrees.

Topping:
1 1/2 cups sour cream
1/4 cup sugar
1 teaspoon vanilla extract

Combine the topping ingredients in a bowl and stir well. Carefully pour or spread over the center of the cheesecake. Return the cheesecake to the 425 degree oven and bake for 7 minutes or until the edge of the topping sets. Remove from the oven and cool to room temperature. Cover loosely with foil and refrigerate for three days. It is very important to complete the full three days before serving.   —Lisa Hall

Decadent Chocolate Chip Cheesecake

May prepare ahead
Serves 10–12

"This easy-to-make cheesecake has proven to be a favorite for all who have tried it and the variations are endless!"

Crust:
2 cups Oreo Cookies, crushed
1/3 cup butter, melted
1/3 cup Kahlua

Filling:
1 cup sour cream
16 ounces ricotta cheese
16 ounces cream cheese, softened
1 1/2 cups sugar
4 eggs, beaten in one at a time
juice of 1 lemon
1 teaspoon vanilla extract
3 tablespoons all-purpose flour
6 ounces mini semisweet chocolate chips

For the crust, mix all three ingredients in a bowl. Then press into the bottom of a large spring form pan. For the filling, mix all of the ingredients in a blender (1/2 at a time), except chocolate chips. Blend until thin and has no lumps. For best results, let cream cheese soften to room temperature before blending. Pour each blender full of batter in the spring form pan over the crust, stirring in half of the mini chocolate chips after each addition. Bake at 350 degrees for 1 hour. Turn temperature off and leave in the oven for 1 more hour. Do not open the oven door. Cool to room temperature, then serve or refrigerate. For chocolate cheesecake, add 3 tablespoons unsweetened cocoa to batter adding more to taste (omitting chocolate chips if desired).
—Shelly Carter

Crazy Cherry Cake

Quick to prepare
Serves 9

"This is my mother's (Gretna T. Vaughn) recipe. We always get raves and recipe requests when served."

1 cup all-purpose flour
1 cup sugar
1 teaspoon baking soda
pinch of salt
1 can pitted pie cherries
1 egg

Sauce:
1 stick butter (no substitute)
1 cup sugar
1/2 cup heavy cream

Sift together flour, sugar, baking soda, and salt. Set aside. Drain the cherries and discard the juice. Add 1 slightly beaten egg to the cherries. Stir into the dry mixture. Pour into a greased 8-inch square pan. Bake at 350 degrees for 50 minutes. Prepare the sauce by melting the butter in the top of a double boiler. Add the sugar and cream. Stir until well heated. Spoon over individual cake servings while warm.

—Mrs. Samuel L. Howe

Grandma's Cold Oven Pound Cake

Freezes well
Serves 8–10

3 cups Swan's Down Cake Flour, sifted
3 cups sugar, sifted
2 sticks margarine
1 cup shortening
1 cup milk
5 eggs
1¹/2 teaspoons vanilla extract
1¹/2 teaspoons lemon extract

Cream sugar, margarine, and shortening. Add the eggs. Add the flour and the milk alternately. Add the flavorings. Mix well with an electric mixer. Bake in cold oven set at 325 degrees for one hour and 20 minutes. For a chocolate pound cake, eliminate the lemon flavoring and add 7 tablespoons cocoa.

Icing:
1 stick margarine
¹/4 cup milk
2 tablespoons cocoa
1 box confectioners' sugar
vanilla extract to taste

Blend all the ingredients until desired consistency.

—Kristie P. Smith

To keep icings moist and to prevent cracking, add a pinch of baking soda to the icing.

Sour Cream Pound Cake

Quick to prepare
Serves 11–12

1 package butter recipe golden cake mix
1 cup (8-ounces) sour cream
1/2 cup oil
1/4 cup sugar
1/4 cup water
4 eggs

Preheat oven to 375 degrees. In a large bowl, blend the cake mix, sour cream, oil, sugar, water and eggs. Beat at high speed for 2 minutes after the ingredients are well-blended. Pour the mix into a greased and floured 10-inch tube pan. May use powdered sugar to flour the pan instead of flour. Bake at 375 degrees for 45 to 55 minutes, or until the cake springs back and looks light brown. Cool for 25 minutes. Then remove from the pan and flip it over to enjoy the powdered sugar glaze.   —Dawn Butler Brooks

Pumpkin Crisp

2 cups cooked pumpkin, or
    1 (16-ounce) can
1 cup evaporated milk
1 cup sugar
1/2 teaspoon cinnamon
3 eggs
1 box yellow cake mix
1 cup chopped nuts
2 sticks butter, melted

Mix first 5 ingredients and pour into a 9x13-inch pan lined with waxed paper. Sprinkle cake mix over these ingredients. Put nuts evenly on top of cake mix and press down. Pour butter evenly over the top. Bake in a 350 degree oven for 50 to 60 minutes.

Topping:
3 ounces cream cheese, softened
3/4 cup cool whip
1 1/2 cups confectioners' sugar

Mix all ingredients together well and spread on top and sides of cooled pumpkin. **Hint: the baked pumpkin mixture needs to be turned upside down after it is baked. The nuts should be on the bottom and pumpkin on top. It's best to remove the waxed paper slowly after it has cooled for about 5 minutes.

—Alice Krawcyzk

Coffee Crunch Parfaits

1 quart coffee ice cream
1 (2¼-ounce) package slivered almonds,
    chopped and toasted, optional, or may
    substitute caramel topping
2 English toffee candy bars, crushed
½ cup chocolate syrup
1 (4-ounce) carton frozen whipped
    topping, thawed
8 maraschino cherries with stems

Spoon ¼ cup ice cream into each of
eight 4-ounce chilled parfait glasses.
Layer ½ teaspoon almonds, optional,
or caramel topping. Layer crushed
candy, chocolate syrup and caramel.
Repeat layers of ice cream, candy,
chocolate. Cover and freeze until
firm. Serve parfait on glass plate.
Pass an assortment of cookies around.
            —Holt Harris

White Chocolate Dream

8 ounces cream cheese, softened
¾ cup confectioners' sugar
1¼ cups whipping cream, divided
3 ounces white chocolate, melted
raspberry sauce

Soften cream cheese. Mix with ¾
cup confectioners' sugar and ¼ cup
whipping cream. Melt chocolate,
use a ziploc bag and microwave in
30 second intervals until smooth,
then cut hole in corner of bag, and
blend into cream cheese mixture.
Whip remaining cream and fold in
mixture. Line a mold with a damp
cheesecloth and put in mixture.
Refrigerate until firm. Unmold,
remove cheesecloth. Serve with
raspberry sauce.   —Amy Boyd

Ice Cream Smores

"Children love the colors of this cool and yummy sandwich—so do adults! It's so easy to make that children can do it themselves."

1 box chocolate graham crackers
1 jar marshmallow cream
1 carton chocolate chip mint ice cream, softened
1 package Hershey's chocolate bars, optional or may substitute Hershey's chocolate syrup

Spread softened ice cream over graham crackers. Spread marshmallow cream over ice cream. Drizzle Hershey's chocolate over marshmallow cream. Top with graham crackers. Place on waxed paper. Cover and freeze.

—Holt A. Harris

Poor Man's Pie

2 cups nuts, pecans or walnuts, chopped
1 (20-ounce) can crushed pineapple, well drained
1 (14-ounce) can sweetened condensed milk
1/2 cup lemon juice
2 (8- or 9-inch) graham cracker pie crusts
1 (12-ounce) container whipped topping

In large bowl mix together nuts, pineapple, milk, lemon juice and topping. Pour into pie crusts and chill several hours.   —Barbara Vaher

When cutting meringue-topped pies or puddings, oil the serving piece. Then the meringue won't tear or pull.

White Chocolate Magnolia Pecan Pie

4 ounces white chocolate, melted
2 eggs
1 can sweetened condensed milk
1 tablespoon white crème de cacao
   liqueur, optional
2 teaspoons vanilla extract
$^1/_3$ cup butter, melted
3 tablespoons milk
$^1/_2$ teaspoon salt
2 cups pecans, chopped
2 regular or 1 deep dish pie shells
pecan halves for garnish

Preheat oven at 425 degrees. Mix ingredients together in order of recipe in large bowl. Pour into pie shells. Garnish pie with pecan halves around the edge of pie shell. Place pies on cookie sheet. Bake at 425 degrees for 12 minutes, then reduce heat to 350 degrees and bake for 30 to 35 minutes.   —Tracy Roberts

Lemonade Quench Pie

1 (16-ounce) can frozen lemonade
   concentrate
1 large container whipped topping
1 small can condensed milk
2 graham cracker pie crusts

Make sure lemonade concentrate has melted to liquid form and whipped topping has melted. Mix both together. Add condensed milk. Mix until all is even. Pour mixture into 2 graham cracker pie crusts evenly. Put lid on pies. Put into freezer and serve after it freezes. Store in the freezer.   —Tifany Gray

Cream Fruit Pie

1 (8-ounce) package cream cheese,
  softened
1 (14-ounce) sweetened condensed milk
1/3 cup lemon juice
1 teaspoon vanilla extract
1 deep dish graham cracker pie crust
assorted fresh fruits (kiwis, strawberries,
  blueberries, grapes, etc.)

Beat cream cheese. Add sweetened
condensed milk and stir. Pour into
ready-made deep dish graham
cracker crust. Chill 3 hours. Arrange
sliced fruit over cream cheese
mixture. I start with sliced strawberries on the outer edge of crust.
Next row, sliced kiwis, then
blueberries filling center.

—Holt A. Harris

Mocha Torte

1 pint coffee ice cream
1 pint butter pecan ice cream
1 pint vanilla ice cream
1 graham cracker pie crust
1 jar Hershey's fudge sauce
salted pecans

Soften and mix coffee, butter pecan,
and vanilla ice cream. Pour into the
pie crust. Freeze for one hour. Spread
hot fudge sauce on top and sprinkle
with salted pecans. Freeze overnight.
—Sue Corbett

Caramel-Apple Pie

6 ounces cream cheese, softened
1 egg
1 1/2 teaspoons vanilla extract
3 tablespoons sugar
1 tablespoon all-purpose flour
1 (12-ounce) package escalloped, frozen,
  apples, defrosted
1/3 cup caramel topping
dash of cinnamon
1 graham cracker pie crust

Preheat oven to 375 degrees.
Combine cream cheese, egg, vanilla,
sugar and flour. Beat until smooth.
Spread mixture over pie crust.
Combine apples, caramel topping
and cinnamon. Gently spoon over
cream cheese mixture to keep 2
distinct layers. Bake for 40 to 45
minutes or until apples bubble up
around edge of pie. Serve at room
temperature and promptly store
leftovers in refrigerator. May use
fat-free or reduced-fat cream cheese.

—Betsy Forbes

Hurry Pie

Makes 2 pies

2 graham cracker crusts
1 (8-ounce) container whipped topping
1 can crushed pineapple
2 tablespoons of lemon juice
1 (14-ounce) can sweetened condensed
   milk

Drain pineapple. Mix with
sweetened milk and lemon juice.
Fold in whipped topping.
Divide mixture evenly into pie
crusts. Refrigerate overnight
before serving.   —Lisa O'Neill

Apple Crumb Pie

2 tablespoons all-purpose flour
1/8 teaspoon salt
3/4 cup sugar
1 egg
1 cup sour cream
1/2 teaspoon vanilla extract
2 cups apples, sliced
1 pastry pie shell

Sift dry ingredients. Add egg,
sour cream and vanilla. Beat until
smooth. Add apples and mix well.
Pour into pastry shell. Bake at
400 to 425 degrees for 15 minutes
and then reduce heat to 350 degrees
for 30 minutes.

Topping:

1/3 cup sugar
1/3 cup all-purpose flour
1 teaspoon cinnamon
1/4 cup butter, softened

Combine ingredients and sprinkle
over pie. Return to oven and bake at
400 degrees for 10 minutes.
                    —Christy Luce

Black Bottom Peanut Butter Chip Pie

1 (9-inch) unbaked pastry shell, bottom
    pricked with fork
1 cup semisweet chocolate pieces
1/3 cup half-and-half
1 (14-ounce) can sweetened condensed
    milk
1 cup peanut butter flavored chips
2 cups whipping cream, stiffly whipped
1/2 cup chopped peanuts

Preheat oven to 425 degrees. Bake pastry shell 10 to 15 minutes or until lightly browned. In 1 quart glass measure with handle, combine chocolate chips with half-and-half. Cook in microwave on high 1 to 2 minutes, stirring until chips are melted and mixture is smooth. Spread evenly on bottom of prepared pastry shell. In 2 quart glass measure with handle, combine sweetened condensed milk and peanut butter chips, cook on high for 2 to 3 minutes, stirring each minute until chips are melted and mixture is smooth. Pour into large bowl; cool to room temperature, about 45 minutes. With mixer, beat until smooth. Fold in whipped cream and peanuts. Chill 30 minutes. Spoon into prepared pastry shell. Chill 4 hours. Garnish as desired. Refrigerate leftovers.

—Kathleen Boyce

Peppermint Pie

This pie is light and refreshing and is a pretty shade of pink.

1 pound peppermint candy
1 (8-ounce) container whipped topping
2 chocolate pie crusts
1 quart milk

Dissolve candy in milk for 24 hours stirring occasionally while in refrigerator. Once candy has dissolved completely, stir in container of cool whip non dairy whipped topping. Pour into 2 chocolate pie crusts and freeze overnight. —Leslie Wallace

Brownie Pie

1 cup sugar
1/4 cup all-purpose flour
1/4 cup cocoa powder
2 eggs, slightly beaten
1 teaspoon vanilla extract
1 stick butter or margarine, melted

Sift sugar, flour and cocoa together. Mix in slightly beaten eggs and vanilla extract. Mix in margarine. Pour into pie shell. Serve with ice cream or whipped topping.
—Robin Hackney

Add a teaspoon of cold water to egg whites while beating to increase the volume.

Holiday & Gift-Giving

Spiced Tea Mix

May prepare ahead
Yields 24 cups

*1/2 cup orange flavored dry instant
    breakfast drink*
1/2 cup instant tea
1/2 cup sugar
1/2 cup lemonade flavored dry drink mix
1/4 teaspoon ground cinnamon
1/3 teaspoon ground cloves

Mix all ingredients. Store in
tightly covered container at room
temperature up to 6 months. For
each serving, place 2 to 3 teaspoons
mix in cup or mug and add 3/4 cup
boiling water. For 6 servings, place
1/3 cup mix in heatproof container
and add 4 1/2 cups boiling water.

—Carolyn Niemeyer

Alan's Red Raspberry Punch

Serve immediately
Serves approximately 20

"Pretty holiday punch. This recipe
comes from Alan Waufle, a great
cook. We served this punch by the
gallons during holiday receptions at
the Gaston County Museum."

*1 (12-ounce) can frozen cran-raspberry
    juice*
1 (12-ounce) can pineapple juice, frozen
*1 (46-ounce) glass jar pink grapefruit
    juice*
1 liter ginger ale
1/2 of a 10 ounce bag frozen raspberries
1 star fruit sliced thin (optional)

Smash frozen pineapple juice in
punch bowl until slushy. Slowly add
other juices and ginger ale. Toss in
frozen raspberries. May also float star
fruit slices as an optional garnish.

—Nan Bridgeman

December Cider

Serves 12

1 (12-ounce) can frozen apple juice
  concentrate
1 (12-ounce) can frozen cranberry apple
  juice concentrate
1 (6-ounce) can frozen lemonade
  concentrate
5 sticks cinnamon
1 teaspoon ground nutmeg
7 whole cloves
1/3 cup rum or cinnamon schnapps

In large kettle combine juices
and 6 (12-ounce) cans of water.
Stir in lemonade, stick cinnamon,
nutmeg and cloves. Bring to a boil.
Reduce heat, cover and simmer for
15 minutes. Remove cloves and
cinnamon before serving. Stir in
rum or schnapps. Serve warm.
Makes about 3 quarts.

—Lindsay Lockett

"Grown-up" Cranberry Salad

Must prepare ahead
Serves 12

"My children know this has wine in
it, hence the title. They really like
it, too!"

2 (3-ounce) packages raspberry jello
1 envelope unflavored gelatin
2 cups hot water
1 (16-ounce) can whole cranberry sauce
1 cup burgundy wine
1 (8³/4-ounce) can crushed pineapple,
  drained
1/2 cup chopped pecans

Topping:
1 envelope Dream Whip
1 (3-ounce) package cream cheese,
  softened
3 tablespoons sugar

Dissolve all gelatin in hot water.
Add cranberry sauce and burgundy
and stir well. Stir in pineapple and
pecans. Pour into ring mold and
refrigerate until firm. To make
topping, prepare whipped topping
mix by directions on envelope.
Mix cream cheese and sugar and
combine with whipped topping.

—Ginger Hinman

Scarborough Fair Leg of Lamb

Must prepare ahead
Serves 10

"Perfect for Easter. The fresh herb marinade gives the lamb a marvelous flavor. Delicious served with roasted potatoes, fresh steamed asparagus, and carrot soufflé."

3 to 4 garlic cloves, minced
1 teaspoon salt
1/2 cup red wine vinegar
1 1/2 cups extra-virgin olive oil
1 teaspoon dry mustard
1 tablespoon coarsely chopped peppercorns
1 tablespoon freshly chopped chives
2 tablespoons freshly chopped parsley
2 tablespoons freshly chopped sage
2 tablespoons freshly chopped rosemary
2 tablespoons freshly chopped thyme
1 (3- to 4-pound) boneless leg of lamb
mint jelly

Preheat oven to 425 degrees. In mixing bowl, combine minced garlic and salt; mash with fork to make a paste. Add vinegar and oil; whisk until well blended. Add herbs and seasonings; mix well. Place lamb in plastic bag, pour in marinade, and seal. Place in pyrex dish and refrigerate 24 hours, turning lamb occasionally. Before roasting, brush herbs and peppercorns from meat. Place in roasting pan and place pan in 425 degree oven. Immediately turn oven heat down to 350 degrees. Roast 20 to 30 minutes per pound until desired degree of doneness is achieved. Serve with mint jelly.

—Kathleen Boyce

Christmas Trifle

Must prepare one day ahead
Serves 8

1 quart milk
2 tablespoons cornstarch
1 cup sugar
dash of salt
8 egg yolks
1 tablespoon vanilla or rose brandy
pound cake (approximately 1/4 cake,
*   bought or homemade)*
raspberry jam
1 can Bing cherries or other
*   sweet cherries*
sherry or rose brandy
whipped cream (optional)

Prepare custard the day before serving: Heat 1 quart milk in top of double boiler. Stir in a mixture of 2 tablespoons cornstarch, 1 cup sugar, and a dash of salt until smoothly blended. Cook for 30 minutes, stirring constantly. Add 8 beaten egg yolks with constant stirring, cooking a few more minutes until thickened. Add 1 tablespoon vanilla or rose brandy. Chill overnight. To assemble trifle: Make little pound cake and raspberry jam "sandwiches". Arrange these sandwiches and cherries around bottom and sides of pretty glass bowl. Sprinkle sherry or rose brandy on each cake sandwich. Spoon custard into bowl. Decorate the top with cake, cherries, and dabs of jam. Chill for several hours. At serving time garnish with whipped cream, if desired.   —Kay Moss

Bake cupcakes in ice cream cones for children by placing cones in muffin tins and filling 2/3 full with batter.

Figgy Pudding (Bread and Butter Fig Pudding with Bourbon Sauce)

Serve warm
Serves 10

"I am always asked to bring this for our Supper Club's Christmas Dinner as well as my family's. It smells so good cooking too! The sauce is so good I sometimes double it."

1 (1-pound) loaf soft Italian or French
    bread without seeds
1 cup butter, softened
1¹/₂ pounds fig preserves or jam (2 cups)
3 eggs
³/₄ cup sugar
1¹/₂ cups milk
1 teaspoon ground cinnamon
1 teaspoon vanilla extract
¹/₂ teaspoon ground nutmeg
¹/₄ cup brown sugar, packed

Bourbon Sauce:
1 cup whipping cream
1 teaspoon vanilla extract
3 egg yolks
1/3 cup sugar
 3 tablespoons bourbon

Lightly butter a 3-quart round casserole. Cut the bread into ¹/₂ inch thick slices. Generously butter both sides of bread slices. Layer ¹/₃ of the bread slices in the bottom of the casserole, overlapping if necessary to fit. Spread half of the fig preserves evenly over bread slices. Layer with another ¹/₃ of bread slices. Spread with remaining preserves and top with remaining bread slices. In a medium mixing bowl beat the eggs and sugar with a wire whisk until well combined. Slowly beat in the milk. Add the cinnamon, vanilla and nutmeg. Pour the egg mixture over the bread. Sprinkle brown sugar over all. Cover casserole with lid or foil. Place casserole in a roasting pan on an oven rack. Pour very hot water into pan around casserole to a depth of one inch. Bake at 375 degrees for 35 minutes. Remove lid or foil. Bake an additional 10 minutes or till set and top is golden brown. Let stand at room temperature 10 to 15 minutes before serving. Serve with Bourbon Sauce: In a medium saucepan combine the whipping cream and the vanilla. Bring just to a boil. Immediately remove the pan from heat. Beat together the egg yolks and sugar. Stir ¹/₂ cup of the hot cream into the egg yolks, stirring constantly. Pour all back into the saucepan. Stir to combine and cook over low heat about 3 minutes or until just bubbly. Cook and stir 2 minutes more. Remove from the heat and stir in the bourbon. Makes about 1 cup of sauce. You can prepare the Bourbon Sauce ahead, but risk a "curdled" look when reheating.

—Ruth Everhart

Stuffed Thanksgiving Pumpkin

Serves 6–8 (or more when used as
a side-dish)

1 small, pretty pumpkin
1 (10-ounce) package frozen tiny peas
1 (9-ounce) package frozen sugar pod
    peas
1 tablespoon butter or olive oil
1/2 to 3/4 cup chopped onion or whole
    pearl onions
3/4 cup sliced mushrooms
1/2 teaspoon dried basil or mint, or
    2 teaspoons fresh chopped basil
    or mint
salt and pepper to taste

Cut lid off pumpkin and clean out seeds. Cook pumpkin and lid in microwave or in oven until pumpkin flesh is barely soft. Check often to avoid overcooking which will cause pumpkin to collapse. I begin with about 8 minutes cooking time in microwave and then cook for several shorter intervals until pumpkin is done. To make stuffing for pumpkin, cook peas and pods according to directions on package. Sauté onion and mushrooms in butter or oil until barely tender. Stir in mint, peas, and pods. Salt and pepper to taste. Fill pumpkin with this mixture. Just before serving, reheat stuffed pumpkin 3 to 4 minutes in microwave. (Longer heating will be required if the pumpkin has been refrigerated.) This looks very pretty, and the pumpkin is delicious scooped out and eaten along with the peas. You may want to invent your own filling for the pumpkin. Cooked apples or pears with cranberries, sugar, and cinnamon make a great alternative stuffing. Or try a combination of cooked meats and vegetables, well-seasoned with pepper and herbs. —Kay Moss

New Year's Pita Bread

Yields: 3 (8–9 inch) pitas

"This pita bread is a Greek tradition. It is served at New Year's. The person who receives the piece with the dime is awarded good luck for the new year. My sister-in-law, Lucy Tuvrides, is a sustainer in the Lakeland, Florida Junior League. She shared this with me and it is now a tradition in our family."

3/4 pound butter
1¹/2 cups sugar
5 eggs, beaten
¹/2 cup orange juice
6 cups all-purpose flour
¹/2 teaspoon baking soda
¹/2 teaspoon baking powder
1 small package slivered almonds
3 dimes wrapped in aluminum foil

Melt butter and let cool. Add sugar, eggs, and orange juice. Mix well. Set aside. In a large mixing bowl, combine flour, baking soda, and baking powder. Add egg mixture to dry ingredients. Mix well. Spread mixture into three 8- or 9-inch round cake pans. Add a wrapped dime to each pan. Press around the edges of each pita with a fork to make a design. Using the slivered almonds, decorate each pita with the man of the house's initials and the date of the new year. Bake for 30 minutes at 350 degrees. Before cutting the bread, designate each piece to a person in the family. The pieces may represent health, good finances, leisure, etc. The person who receives the piece with a dime is awarded good luck for the new year. Be careful when eating the bread due to the fact that it contains a dime. Do not reheat bread in the microwave.   —Julie Heath

Cheese Ball with Marinated Dried Tomatoes

Prepare ahead
Yields 6 (¹/₂ cup) gifts

3 (8-ounce) packages cream cheese,
    softened
1 (7-ounce) jar oil-packed dried
    tomatoes, drained
1 garlic clove
2 teaspoons dried basil
¹/₂ cup coarsely chopped pine nuts or
    almonds, toasted

Position knife blade in food processor
bowl; add first 4 ingredients. Process
until smooth. Cover and chill at least
3 hours. Shape ¹/₂ cup mixture into
a ball; roll in toasted pine nuts or
almonds, pressing gently to make
nuts adhere. Repeat procedure with
remaining mixture and nuts. Wrap
each ball in plastic wrap. Chill. Store
in refrigerator up to 5 days. Serve
with unsalted crackers. Package
cheese ball in a decorated terra cotta
pot. Wrap ball in clear plastic, tie
with a bow, nestled in a fabric-lined
pot. Can also use plastic plant tray
down in terra cotta pot then place
the cheese ball and wrap entire pot
with cellophane. May also add a
larger terra cotta saucer to be used
for chips or crackers.

—Carolyn Niemeyer

Rose Brandy Flavoring

Prepare ahead
Yields as much as desired

"You may find yourself adding
heritage rose varieties to your garden
especially for their use in making
this flavoring. Fresh rose petals also
add a lovely garnish to a sweet salad,
dessert, beverages, or party sandwiches. Damask roses and the
Gallicas are my favorites for late
spring bloom and for making rose
brandy. Old Blush is a nice variety
for yielding occasional blooms in the
the summer and early fall."

fragrant rose petals (avoid those that
    have been sprayed with poisons!)
brandy

Pick fragrant rose petals and pack
into a jar. Pour on just enough
brandy to cover. Allow to set for
1 to 2 days. Strain off the brandy,
discard used petals, and pour the
brandy over fresh rose petals. Repeat
3-4 times, using fresh petals but
the same brandy each time, until
the brandy has extracted a strong
fragrance from the roses. Store the
resulting rose flavoring in a tightly
capped container. Use in cakes,
cookies, and puddings for a delicious
change from plain vanilla. I like to
double the amount of flavoring in
pound cakes and custards, whether
I use vanilla or this wonderful
rose brandy.   —Kay Moss

Sweet Butters

May prepare ahead
Keep chilled
Yields 1 cup

"This makes a nice gift when given along with a loaf of homemade bread."

Beat 1 cup (2 sticks) butter, softened, and one of the following:

Almond: 2 tablespoons finely chopped almonds, and 1 teaspoon almond extract

Orange: 2 teaspoons grated orange peel and 2 tablespoons orange juice

Raspberry: 1 cup raspberries, crushed and 2 tablespoons sugar or 1/2 cup raspberry jam

Store tightly covered in refrigerator up to 3 weeks or in freezer up to 2 months. For easy slicing, shape butter into a log and wrap tightly in plastic wrap or waxed paper before storing.

—Carolyn Niemeyer

Fig Conserve

Must prepare ahead
Yield 4 pints

4 pounds figs, chopped
3 pounds sugar
1/2 box white or golden raisins
1/2 cup chopped pecans
1 whole orange, chopped
juice of one lemon

Cook figs and sugar until figs are soft and amber colored. Add remaining ingredients; cook until thickened, stirring constantly. Pack in hot jars. Set jars, with tightened lids, in hot water bath for 15 minutes.

—Meg Farmer

Savory Butters

May prepare ahead
Freezes well
Yields 1 cup

"These flavored butters are delicious with fresh bread, and they also are excellent on vegetables. You can also use them to baste meat, poultry or fish when broiling or baking."

Beat 1 cup (2 sticks) butter, softened and one of the following:

Garlic: 2 teaspoons paprika, 1/2 teaspoon pepper and 8 cloves garlic, crushed

Herb: 1/4 to 1/2 cup chopped fresh or 1 to 2 tablespoons dried herb (basil, chives, oregano, savory, tarragon or thyme)

1 tablespoon lemon juice and 1/4 teaspoon salt

Store tightly covered in refrigerator up to 3 weeks or in freezer up to 2 months. You can also place on waxed paper and roll into a log, twist each end and tie with ribbon. When ready to use just slice and place on bread, vegetables or as a basting for meat.

—Carolyn Niemeyer

"Red Meat" Seasoning

Keeps well
Yields 1/3 cup

"Using tablespoons will make 2 to 3 bottles that can be given as gifts."

7 teaspoons onion powder
4 teaspoons black pepper
3 teaspoons garlic powder
2 teaspoons ground ginger
1 teaspoon sugar
1 teaspoon ground paprika
1/2 teaspoon celery seed

Mix all ingredients together in a mixing bowl. Transfer mix to an empty spice bottle with a shaker top for use. Mix with ground beef for hamburger patties. Sprinkle on steaks, roasts, stews, or meatloaves for seasoning.   —Lisa Thomas

Chocolate-Mint Dessert Spread

Must prepare ahead
Yields 3 gifts

1¹/2 cups (9 ounces) semisweet chocolate
    chips, melted
¹/2 cup crème de menthe liqueur
3 (8-ounce) packages cream cheese,
    softened
1 teaspoon ground cinnamon
2 cups finely chopped pecans
Chocolate cookie wafers to serve

In a large bowl, mix together first
4 ingredients until smooth. Cover
and chill for 1 hour. Divide mixture
into thirds and form into balls. Roll
balls in pecans. Serve with chocolate
cookie wafers. Store in refrigerator.

—Carolyn Niemeyer

No Fuss Caramel Corn

May prepare ahead
Makes 3 quarts

"This is a great gift idea for any
holiday. Just fill the tin full of No
Fuss Caramel Corn and they will
return it for a refill."

3 quarts popped corn
1¹/2 cups peanuts
1 cup brown sugar, packed
¹/2 cup butter
¹/4 cup light corn syrup
¹/2 teaspoon salt
¹/2 teaspoon baking soda

Pop corn in hot air popper, if
available. Place popped corn and
peanuts in large brown paper bag.
Set aside. Combine brown sugar,
butter, corn syrup and salt in a
2-quart glass bowl. Microwave on
high setting for 3 to 4 minutes,
stirring after each minute, until
mixture comes to a boil. Microwave
2 minutes more. Stir in baking soda.
Pour syrup mixture over popped
corn and peanuts in bag. Close bag
and shake well. Microwave on high
setting for 1¹/2 minutes. Shake bag
well. Microwave 1¹/2 minutes more.
Shake bag and pour caramelized
popcorn into a large roasting pan.
Cool and stir to separate corn
kernels.   —Leslie Wallace

Gabriel's Horns

Great for a cookie party for
children!

1 box of bugles
creamy peanut butter
melted chocolate

Spread peanut better in the open end
of bugle. Dip peanut buttered end
into chocolate. Lay on waxed paper
to dry. Store in air tight container, or
package in cellophane bags tied
with ribbon.   —Carolyn Niemeyer

Maple Syrup

May prepare ahead
Yields 2¹/₂ cups

"This makes a nice gift to put into
a food basket along with a pancake
mix. Just pour syrup into a pretty
glass jar with a tightly sealed lid
and tie with a ribbon."

2 cups sugar
1 cup water
1 teaspoon lemon juice (prevents
*   crystallization)*
³/4 teaspoon maple extract

Bring sugar, water and lemon juice
to a boil. Add extract and remove
from heat. Serve warm over pancakes
or french toast.   —Leslie Wallace

Before party guests arrive, scoop ice cream into muffin tins lined with cupcake liners
and refreeze. Then you won't have to wait for ice cream to soften before scooping!

Chocolate Peanut Clusters

May prepare ahead
Yields 5 dozen candies

"Men love this candy!"

2 pounds white chocolate
1 (12-ounce) bag semisweet chocolate
    morsels
3 tablespoons cocoa
1 tablespoon vegetable oil
2 (1 pound) cans cocktail peanuts

Melt white chocolate, semisweet chocolate morsels, cocoa, and oil in a crock pot or double boiler. Stir in peanuts. Drop by teaspoonful onto wax paper. Let cool. Store in airtight container or place in individual tins or bags for gift giving. —Lisa Rouse

Hot Chocolate Mix

May prepare ahead
Yield: 2 cups

3/4 cup sugar
1/4 cup blanched almonds
1/2 cup unsweetened cocoa powder
1 teaspoon ground cinnamon
1/2 teaspoon instant espresso coffee powder
    (optional)
3.2 ounce nonfat dry milk (enough to
    make 1 quart)

Combine the sugar and almonds in blender or food processor and process for several minutes into a smooth paste. Add the cocoa, cinnamon, instant espresso, and nonfat dry milk. Process for 1 minute more. Store in an airtight container. Will keep for several months. To package: Present the Hot Chocolate Mix in a decorative airtight tin with a tag giving the directions for making into hot chocolate. For each cup of hot chocolate, bring 3/4 cup water or milk to a simmer, add 1/4 cup hot chocolate mix and simmer. Whisk constantly for 30 seconds. Top with whipped cream or marshmallows.
                    —Carolyn Niemeyer

Flavored Vinegars

Prepare ahead
Yields 4–5 cups

"These bottles make beautifully decorated and impressive Christmas gifts."

4 cups white, distilled vinegar
1/2 cup sugar

Choice of following combinations:
pineapple tidbits with orange peel
whole spring onions with garlic bit
fresh whole cranberries with orange peel
lemon peel, garlic bits, and whole cloves
blueberries with lemon peel
raspberries with lemon peel
whole red chile peppers

Mix vinegar and sugar. Choose glass containers with cork lids. Fill container 1/3 full with choice of combinations listed above. Amounts may vary as you wish. However, it is recommended to use no more than 1 teaspoon of garlic bits since they tend to overpower other ingredients. Cover ingredients with vinegar/sugar mixture. Top container with cork. Dip lid of container in melted paraffin to seal. —Patricia Ratchford

Dustpan Snack Mix

May prepare ahead
Serves 12–15

1 (10.5-ounce) package of corn chips
1 (10-ounce) package of pretzels
1 (7-ounce) package of cheese stick
  crackers
2 cups oyster crackers
3 ounces honey roasted peanuts
3 ounces salty peanuts
3/4 cup melted margarine
6 ounces frozen limeade, thawed
1 3/4 ounces chili seasoning

Preheat oven to 250 degrees.
In a large pan, combine first six
ingredients. In a small bowl,
combine melted butter, limeade and
chili mix; stir until blended. Pour
over snack mixture, stir until well
coated. Bake for 1 hour, stirring
every 15 minutes. Spread mixture
on foil to cool. Store in an airtight
container.   —Kathy Plemmons

Maggie's Cheese Ball

"This recipe makes 4 cheese balls—
great for gifts!"

5 (8-ounce) packages cream cheese,
  softened
2 tablespoons minced onion
1/2 cup mayonnaise
1 1/2 inches of Hostess ham, chopped
  finely
12 shakes of hot sauce
2 cups of shredded cheese (sharpness
  depending on taste)
1 1/2 cups chopped pecans

Combine first six ingredients.
Form into cheese balls. Roll in
pecans. Serve with assorted crackers.
This cheese ball was "the talk of
Duke Power".   —Robin Hackney

Blowing Rock Salad Dressing

May prepare ahead
Yields 6 cups

1 cup seedless raspberry preserves
1/3 cup honey
1 cup red wine vinegar
1/2 cup lemon juice
1 1/2 cups vegetable oil
1 tablespoon poppy seed
1 teaspoon salt

Put all of the above ingredients in a blender. Blend 40 seconds until mixture has a pink creamy appearance. Pour in glass containers. This may be refrigerated—lasts weeks in refrigerator. This is a wonderful idea for quick gifts. Just add a ribbon—put in a pretty decanter. This makes enough for six small containers, three medium or two large glass bottles.

—Janie Parks Peak

Microwave Peanut Brittle

Serves 4

1 1/2 cups raw shelled peanuts (skins on)
1 cup sugar
1/2 cup light corn syrup
1/8 teaspoon salt
1 teaspoon butter
1 teaspoon vanilla extract
1 teaspoon baking soda

In a 1 1/2 quart microwaveable container, stir together peanuts, sugar, syrup, and salt. Cook 8 minutes on high in microwave oven stirring well after 4 minutes. Stir in butter and vanilla. Microwave 2 minutes longer on high. Add baking soda and quickly stir until foamy. Immediately pour onto lightly greased baking sheet; spreading the batter quickly. Allow to cool for at least 30 minutes. Break into small pieces. Store in tin container.

—Patricia Ratchford

Chocolate-Covered Pretzel Mix

20 ounces white almond bark
1 (10-ounce) bag of mini pretzels
 (curly)
1 (16-ounce) bag of chocolate candies
 (M&M's)

Prepare white almond bark as directed on the package. Immediately add pretzels. Continue to stir with rubber spatula until all pretzels are covered. Add chocolate candies (red and green if it is Christmas time). Stir and pour onto wax paper. Spread them apart to harden. This mix will be ready to put into tins in about 5 minutes. Don't worry if the pretzels stick together. They still taste great!

—Julie Heath

Forget-Ems

Must prepare ahead
Yields 2–2 1/2 dozen

3 egg whites
1 cup of sugar
1 (12-ounce) bag of semisweet chocolate
 morsels

Line oven rack with aluminum foil. Preheat oven to 350 degrees. Beat egg whites until stiff. Add sugar to egg whites slowly. Fold in semisweet chocolate morsels. If desired fold in a few drops of food coloring for a holiday cookie. Drop mixture by teaspoonfuls on foil-lined oven rack. Close oven. Turn oven off and "forget-em." Cookies will be ready in the morning.

—Cherie Montgomery Furr

Homemade Vanilla

Must prepare ahead
Yields approximately 2 cups

4 vanilla beans, good quality
2 cups cognac, best you can afford

Cut beans crosswise into 3 or 4 pieces. Split each piece open lengthwise, but do not cut through. Place in jar and pour cognac over and seal tightly. Let stand 2 to 4 weeks. Strain into smaller bottles for gifts and add a piece of vanilla bean to each bottle. Store in cool, dark place. As it is used, it can be replenished by adding more cognac and allowing it to stand before using.

—Lisa Thomas

Cheese Cookies

Yields 125 cookies

"A Christmas tradition in our family. This is not a "cheese straw" tasting cookie. This recipe was used at the Junior League Christmas Cookie Exchange."

1 pound butter (do not substitute
  margarine)
1/2 cup sugar
5 cups all-purpose flour
1 egg yolk
3 cups grated sharp cheddar cheese
Sugar in a dish to use for rolling cookies
  in after baking

Melt butter. Cream in sugar. Fold in flour. Add egg yolk and mix well. Knead in cheese. Form dough into small balls and place on an ungreased cookie sheet. Use thumb to make a dent in the top of each ball. Bake at 350 degrees for 8 to 12 minutes. Do not brown! Roll in sugar while hot.

—Jo Gray

Playdough

May prepare ahead
Makes 9–10 party favors

2 cups all-purpose flour
2 cups water
1 cup salt
2 tablespoons cooking oil
2 teaspoons cream of tartar
Food coloring to tint if desired

Combine all ingredients in a large pot over low heat. Cook, stirring constantly, until dough forms. Remove from heat and let cool. Store in airtight containers. Variation: Josie Conner uses this for children's party favors and/or gift giving. Place a small amount in a ziploc bag. Attach a desired shape cookie cutter. Cinnamon or peppermint extract can be added during the cooking stage for a wonderful Christmas smell.

—Lisa Thomas

Cinnamon Ornaments

Must prepare ahead
Makes 10–12 ornaments

"This is a great project for children to make scented cinnamon ornaments for their own tree or as a special gift."

1 cup cinnamon
1 tablespoon cloves
1 tablespoon nutmeg
3/4 cup applesauce
2 tablespoons white glue

Mix and roll out to 1/4-inch thickness on waxed paper or aluminum foil. Use cookie cutters to cut into desired shapes, smaller shapes tend to work better. Pierce a small hole near top of ornament. Allow to dry for one day. May need to be flipped over to complete drying process. Tie red narrow ribbon through the hole, and use as Christmas ornaments.

—Susan Allen

Finger Paint

Washable
Yields 2–2½ cups

"Great idea for children's birthday party."

2 tablespoons sugar
¹/3 cup cornstarch
2 cups cold water
¹/4 cup liquid dishwashing soap

Mix sugar and cornstarch in saucepan, slowly adding cold water. Cook over low heat for 5 minutes, stirring constantly until the mixture is a clear smooth gel. When cool, stir in liquid dishwashing soap. Scoop into plastic containers and stir in desired amount of dry tempera paint. To give as a party favor, put in small containers and wrap finger paint paper around container and tie with ribbon.   —Josie Conner

Bubble Solution

May prepare ahead
Yields 8³/4 cups

"This recipe makes great bubbles!"

2 cups Joy or Dawn dish detergent
6 cups of water
³/4 cup light corn syrup

Mix ingredients together. Use to refill all those small bubble bottles or pour in pan for use with a giant bubble wand.   —Beth Brittain

Dog Biscuits

May prepare ahead
Makes approximately 36 biscuits

"Bo gives these to his "dog" friends at Christmas. All dogs love them!"

2 teaspoons chicken bouillon
1 cup boiling water
1 cup rolled oats
1/2 cup margarine
3/4 cup cornmeal
1 tablespoon sugar
1/2 cup milk
1 egg
1 cup cheddar cheese
3 cups whole wheat flour
1 teaspoon garlic powder

Dissolve bouillon in boiling water. Add all other ingredients and mix well. Roll out about 1/2 inch thick. Cut with a dog bone cutter. Place on a greased cookie sheet and bake 45 minutes at 350 degrees. If you want them to have a shiny appearance, you can brush them with egg.

—Cheryl Black

Homemade Kahlúa

May prepare ahead
Makes 7 cups

1 quart water
2 1/2 cups sugar
3 tablespoons instant coffee
1 tablespoon vanilla extract
2 1/2 cups vodka

Bring water, sugar and coffee to a boil in a saucepan. Simmer very slowly for 3 hours. Mixture will be very dark and syrupy. Cool. Add vanilla and vodka. Serve as an after-dinner liqueur or over vanilla ice cream. Bottle in carafes or decorative bottles for gifts.   —Lindsay Lockett

The Perfect Pancake Mix

Yields: 7¹/2 cups mix or 15 (5-pancake) batches

"This is a great mix to use in a gift basket with flavored syrups and/or butters!"

3 cups all-purpose flour
1 tablespoon baking soda
4¹/2 teaspoons baking powder
1¹/2 teaspoons salt
1 tablespoon sugar (optional)
*2 cups whole wheat or oat flour, or a
    combination*
*1 cup seven whole grain cereal
    (available at health food stores)*
1 cup cornmeal
4 tablespoons wheat germ (optional)

In a large mixing bowl, sift the all-purpose flour with the baking soda, baking powder, salt, and optional sugar. Drop in the remaining flour, cereal, cornmeal, and wheat germ and stir until thoroughly blended. Store in an airtight container and, if using wheat germ, refrigerate. Type or print the directions on a card to give with mix.

Perfect Pancakes

"You can store leftover batter in the refrigerator for two days and reheat leftover pancakes in a toaster."

1 tablespoon butter
1 egg
*¹/2 cup nonfat yogurt, buttermilk, sour
    cream, or milk*
¹/2 cup Perfect Pancake Mix

Set a griddle or skillet over medium heat and melt butter. Lightly beat the egg with the yogurt, buttermilk, sour cream, or milk. Add the pancake mix and stir just until smooth. Ladle the batter onto the skillet. Turn the pancakes when you see air bubbles on the surface (about 1 minute). Serve with maple syrup, jam, yogurt, or confectioner sugar. Makes about 5 medium pancakes.

—Tammy Sasser

Pretzels

Best if served warm
May prepare ahead
Yields: 8 pretzels

1 package dry yeast
1¹/₂ cups warm water
1 teaspoon salt
1 teaspoon sugar
4 cups all-purpose flour
coarse salt
1 egg yolk, beaten

Preheat oven to 425 degrees. Pour the water into the mixing bowl, add the yeast, and dissolve it. Once the yeast is dissolved, add 1 teaspoon of salt, then add the sugar and flour. Knead the dough until the mixture is smooth. If the dough is sticky, add a little more flour until it feels drier. Take out little bits about the size of a walnut, and roll them into a ball. On the breadboard, roll the balls into long ropes (about 12 inches long). Shape the ropes into pretzel shapes, or other desired shapes. Place pretzels on baking sheet. Brush a little egg on top of each pretzel, and sprinkle coarse salt over the egg. Bake at 425 degrees for 15 to 18 minutes.

—Britte Conner

Flavored Cream Cheeses

May prepare ahead

"A great gift idea to go along with homemade pretzels or your favorite bagels."

4 ounces cream cheese, softened
1 tablespoon yogurt, ricotta cheese, or
  sour cream

In a bowl mix cream cheese with yogurt, ricotta cheese, or sour cream until smooth. Add choice of flavorings listed below:

Veggie Cream Cheese:
Add 1 tablespoon each of diced carrots, snipped chives, and diced onion

Strawberry Cream Cheese:
Add 6 to 8 chopped, fresh strawberries

Cinnamon and Raisin Cream Cheese:
Add ¹/₂ teaspoon cinnamon and 2 tablespoons raisins

Sun-Dried Tomato:
Add 2 tablespoons chopped sun-dried tomato with ¹/₂ teaspoon olive oil and a dash of salt (omit the yogurt or other dairy product for softening the spread)

—Britte Conner

Festive Cardamom Twist

Yields 2 loaves

"Our Christmas holidays wouldn't seem complete if my mother, Kay Friesen, didn't make this especially pretty and delicious bread. It is unlike anything else I've tried and is certainly one of our favorite family traditions."

1 package yeast
$1/2$ cup warm water
$2^1/2$ cups milk, scalded and cooled
1 egg
$1/2$ teaspoon salt
1 cup sugar
$1^1/2$ teaspoons ground cardamom
7 cups all-purpose flour (approximately)
Red candied cherries, halved

In a large bowl, blend yeast and water and allow to stand 5 minutes. Stir in the next 5 ingredients until well blended. With heavy spoon stir in most of the 7 cups of flour, enough to form a stiff ball. Knead dough about 10 minutes, adding flour as needed. Set aside, cover and allow to rise for $1^1/2$ to 2 hours. Punch the dough down and on a floured board, separate dough into 6 equal balls. Roll each ball into long ropes (approximately 2 inches around). Take three of the ropes and braid together, repeating with the remaining three. Cover and set the two braided loaves in a warm place and allow to rise another $1^1/2$ to 2 hours (until the loaves double in size). Bake at 350 degrees for 35 to 40 minutes or until golden brown. Drizzle the loaves with glaze.

Glaze:
2 cups confectioners' sugar
4 tablespoons milk
1 teaspoon lemon extract

Mix ingredients in saucepan and heat thoroughly, stirring constantly.
—Shelly F. Carter

Peanut Butter Ghost Cookies

May prepare ahead
Makes approximately 30 cookies

"Can be made with the kids' help. Great for a Halloween party at home or school."

1 package "Nutter Butter" peanut shaped cookies
1 package Baker's block white chocolate
1 small box of raisins

Melt the chocolate over medium heat in a double boiler until just melted, but do not overcook. Once melted, dip one end of each cookie in the chocolate and place on waxed paper. Use the raisins to make the eyes. Let stand until chocolate has cooled and hardened. Keep in an airtight container.
—Lisa King

Granny B's Persimmon Pudding

Prepare ahead
Serves 12–15

"My granny's all-time specialty and my all-time favorite!"

1¹/2 cups sugar
2 cups milk
1¹/2 cups self-rising flour
1 teaspoon baking soda
1 teaspoon baking powder
1 teaspoon cinnamon
¹/4 teaspoon cloves
¹/4 teaspoon allspice
¹/2 teaspoon salt
3 eggs
2 teaspoons vanilla extract
¹/2 cup butter, softened
2 cups persimmon pulp
1 cup grated sweet potato

Sift all dry ingredients together. Add to all other ingredients. Put in 9x13-inch pan and bake for 1 hour at 300 degrees.

—Mrs. Phillip J. Nixon

Salted Peanut Chews

Prepare ahead
Yields 36 bars, depending on size

1 package yellow cake mix
¹/3 cup margarine, softened
1 egg
3 cups miniature marshmallows
²/3 cup white corn syrup
¹/4 cup margarine
2 teaspoons vanilla extract (I use pure vanilla extract, but imitation is fine too)
2 cups peanut butter chips
2 cups Rice Krispies cereal
2 cups salted peanuts

Preheat oven to 350 degrees. Mix cake mix, ¹/3 cup margarine and egg by hand or in a mixer on low speed until crumbly. Press onto just the bottom of an ungreased 9x13-inch pan. Bake until golden brown about 13 minutes. Remove and immediately sprinkle with marshmallows. Return to oven for 1 to 2 minutes until marshmallows just begin to puff. Remove from oven and cool. Heat together the corn syrup, ¹/4 cup margarine, vanilla, and peanut butter chips. Heat until melted and smooth, stirring occasionally. Remove from heat. Stir in rice cereal and peanuts. Spoon mixture over marshmallow cover crust. Spread evenly.

—Candy Grooms

Homemade Tortilla Chips

"These would be great in a gift basket along with salsa and/or guacamole. A great summer idea for new neighbors!"

8 (8-inch) flour tortillas
8 tablespoons olive oil
Coarse salt

Preheat oven to broil. Cut each tortilla into 8 wedges and lightly brush both sides with the oil. Arrange them on a jellyroll pan. Broil, flipping once when they begin to brown. When brown on both sides, remove and lightly sprinkle with salt.

Variations:

Herb Tortillas:
Add 1 tablespoon chopped fresh herbs (parsley, cilantro, basil, or dill) to the oil, then brush on tortillas.

Garlic Chips:
Crush 1 clove of garlic and add to oil before brushing on tortillas.

Parmesan Chips:
Instead of salt, sprinkle with 1 to 2 teaspoons grated Parmesan cheese.

—Josie Conner

Fresh Salsa

Yields 3 cups

2 garlic cloves
4 jalapeño peppers, sliced in half, seeded,
and veined
1 medium onion, quartered or 1 bunch
of scallions, chopped
¼ cup cilantro leaves
2 large tomatoes or 6 small ones, cored
and quartered

Chop the above ingredients in a food processor with the blades running, turning the machine off between additions (avoid liquifying the tomatoes). If you plan to store the sauce in the refrigerator, place it in a jar and pour a tablespoon of oil over the top.　　—Lindsay Lockett

Chunky Guacamole

Yields: 4 cups

3 ripe avocados, peeled and diced, one pit
reserved
2 tablespoons fresh lime juice
1 cup Fresh Salsa

Sprinkle the chopped avocado with lime juice, stir in the salsa, and place the mixture in a bowl lined with lettuce leaves. If you don't plan to serve it immediately, place an avocado pit in the bowl to prevent browning and cover it tightly with plastic wrap. Store in the refrigerator.
　　　　　　—Susan R. Schultz

Southern Inspirations

*For forty years, League members have volunteered for a better
Gaston County. In our "First Course," we have had great leadership by
an incredible group of ladies. Each has made unique contributions
to the character and direction of our broad and significant service and
financial support to our community. A special thanks to them for their
willingness to move us forward as a strong, committed organization.*

*Forty years ago, eleven women began our league with the purpose of
training members to become responsible citizens and effective community participants.
The challenge is still there today and will be there in the future. The
excitement and commitment to meet that challenge is what keeps the Junior League of
Gaston County thriving. As we begin our "Second Course" of League history, we
have a focus on children's issues and needs. Directing our energy and resources
towards these vital issues will challenge us to positively influence tomorrow's volunteer
leaders. Today, we salute the strong women who have paved the way to our
future as our true "Southern Inspirations."*

—Mrs. Paul L. Heath
(Julie Gray)
President 1998-1999

Mother's Fruit Tea

May prepare ahead
Serves 20

"Although the red cover has long been lost, I still have my Mother's copy of the Greensboro Junior League, circa 1945, a year or so before I became a provisional there. I've never been fond of plain iced tea, probably because Mother kept a big jar of this refreshing tea in the refrigerator all summer long!"

1 quart strong hot tea
2 cups sugar
1 teaspoon whole cloves
1 (46-ounce) can pineapple juice
1 (46-ounce) can grapefruit juice
1 (12-ounce) can frozen concentrate orange juice
1 (6-ounce) can tangerine juice or if unavailable, 1(6-ounce) can frozen orange and tangerine juice

Pour 1 quart, strong hot tea over 2 cups sugar and dissolve. In a saucepan combine 1 teaspoon whole cloves and 1 pint boiling water and boil for 10 minutes. Strain. Add cloves to tea. Add pineapple juice, grapefruit juice, orange juice, and tangerine juice. Mix well. This can be served hot or cold.

—Mrs. J. Clay Williamson
(Betty Kerr Hendrix)
President 1960–1961

Ginger Ale Salad

Must prepare ahead

1 (3.5-ounce) package lemon Jell-O
1 cup ginger ale
1/2 cup grapes, cut in half
1 (15-ounce) can Bartlett pears, cut in small pieces
1/2 cup pecan halves, chopped
1 tablespoon crystallized ginger, crushed
2 tablespoons mayonnaise
1 tablespoon sour cream
dash of ginger, optional

Dilute lemon Jell-O into 1 cup ginger ale. Mix in grapes, pears, pecans and crushed ginger. Pour mixture into a salad mold and refrigerate until congealed. Mix mayonnaise, sour cream and ginger thoroughly and use as a dressing on top of the salad when serving.

"There was a crisis between the U.S. and Cuba. We were all terrified and we went to the City Council to make sure that we had a bomb shelter."

—Mrs. Frank Matthews
(Betty Choate)
President 1961–1962

Classic Brunswick Stew

May prepare ahead
Serves 12–16

"My husband, Harold, and I make this every year. It has become a family tradition in our home. The vinegar in this dish gives it real ZIP and I like to serve it with slaw and cornbread."

1 (3-pound) chicken
1 pound lean beef
1 pound lean pork
3 medium onions, chopped
salt and pepper
water to cover
4 (14.5-ounce) cans tomatoes
5 tablespoons Worcestershire sauce
21 ounces ketchup (1¹/2 bottles)
dash hot pepper sauce
2 bay leaves
6 ounces chili sauce
1 teaspoon dry mustard
¹/2 stick unsalted butter
3 tablespoons vinegar
2 (14.5-ounce) cans small butter beans
2 (14.5-ounce) cans cream style corn
1 (14.5-ounce) can small English peas
3 small, diced Irish potatoes
1 box frozen okra, optional

Put meat in a large, heavy pot and season with salt and pepper. Add onions and cover with water. Cook on medium heat until meat falls from the bones. This will take several hours. Remove from heat and allow to cool. Remove meat from bone.

Tear meat into small shreds and return to stock. Add tomatoes, Worcestershire sauce, ketchup, hot sauce, bay leaves, chili sauce, dry mustard and butter. Cook on medium heat for one hour stirring occasionally to prevent sticking. Adjust heat as needed to avoid scorching. Add vinegar, butter beans, corn, peas, potatoes and okra, if desired. Reduce heat to low and cook slowly until thick.

—Mrs. Harold T. Sumner
(Carolyn Warren)
President 1962–1963

Sweet Potato Casserole

Serves 8

"This recipe is given in loving memory of Betsy Garland by her family. She was a wonderful hostess who loved to entertain family and friends."

6 medium size sweet potatoes
¹/2 cup margarine, melted
¹/2 cup brown sugar, packed
¹/3 cup orange juice
¹/3 cup bourbon
¹/2 teaspoon salt
¹/2 teaspoon pumpkin pie spice
1¹/2 cups chopped pecans

Boil potatoes until tender, peel and mash. Combine with next six ingredients. Spoon into baking dish. Sprinkle pecans over top to cover.

Bake at 375 degrees for 45 minutes. For larger group, add two more potatoes and increase orange juice and bourbon.

—Mrs. James Boyce Garland
(Betsy Matthews)
President 1959–1960

Mushroom, Walnut and Gruyère in Phyllo

Freezes well
Serves 10

3 tablespoons butter
2 tablespoons finely chopped shallots
1 pound chopped mushrooms
1 teaspoon salt
1 teaspoon pepper
1 teaspoon each of fresh tarragon,
  marjoram, oregano, and chives
1/2 cup dry white wine
1/2 cup finely chopped scallions
1/3 cup minced parsley
1 tablespoon lemon juice
1 1/3 cups walnuts, lightly toasted and
  finely chopped
1/2 pound grated Gruyère cheese
  (about 2 cups)
1 package phyllo pastry

Melt butter. Add shallots, mushrooms, salt, pepper, and herbs. Cook over medium heat until most of the liquid has evaporated. Add the wine and cook until evaporate, stirring occasionally. Remove from heat and put into a bowl. Stir in the scallions, parsley and lemon juice. Let cool and add walnuts and cheese, blend thoroughly and set aside. The phyllo package comes with approximately 16 sheets, take off half the sheets and brush each one with melted butter. Stack them to make one unit (the package will make 2 units). With short side facing you, spread filling, leaving 1/2 inch border. Turn edges in so filling doesn't fall out. Roll up tightly. Cut into 1/2 inch slices. Bake at 400 degrees for 12 minutes. Filling makes at least enough for 2 rolls, if there is extra filling freeze for the next time.

"As the first Chairman of the Antique Fair, we made so much hot chicken salad and vegetable soup that we could make it in our sleep."

—Mrs. Lawrence S. Rankin, Jr.
(Lila Spilman)

Raisin Bread Pudding with Whisky Sauce

Serves 6

"Make in your microwave and it is so easy!"

7 slices raisin bread, cubed
1/4 cup brown sugar, packed
1/4 teaspoon salt
2 cups milk
1/4 cup butter, cut in pieces

Whisky Sauce:
1/3 cup sugar
2 tablespoons bourbon
1/4 cup butter, cut in pieces
1 egg, beaten

Spread bread cubes in 6x10-inch glass baking dish. Sprinkle with brown sugar and salt. Microwave milk and butter on high in 4 cup glass measure until hot, about 4 minutes. Whisk in eggs; pour over bread cubes. Microwave on high 9 minutes, or until knife inserted in center comes out clean, turning once. For whisky sauce, mix sugar and bourbon in 2 cup glass measure; stir in butter. Microwave on high 2 minutes or until mixture is bubbly. Stir some sauce mixture into egg; pour egg back into bourbon mixture and whisk until smooth. Serve warm over bread pudding.

—Mrs. W.D. Lawson, III
(Betsy Smith)
President 1963–1964
President 1964–1965

Green Rice

Serve immediately
Serves 6–8

"A family favorite given to me during League days by Mary Lytle, an excellent cook and friend."

1 cup uncooked rice
1 cup half-and-half
salt as desired
1/3 cup canola oil
1 cup grated sharp cheddar cheese
1 chopped green bell pepper
1 medium onion, chopped
1/2 garlic clove, mashed
2/3 cup chopped fresh parsley
1 beaten egg

Cook rice as usual. Mix rice with all other ingredients except egg. Test for salt before egg is added. Add egg and pour into greased casserole. At this point the casserole can be covered and refrigerated until one hour before cooking. Place casserole in pan of hot water and bake 35 to 40 minutes at 325 degrees. Texture is soufflé like. Excellent served with beef or baked fish.

—Mrs. Giles D. Beal, Jr.
(Martha Barnett)
President 1965–1966

Crab Delight

May prepare ahead
Serves 4

"This quick and easy to prepare dish is both rich and delicious!"

1 pound lump crab meat
2 tablespoons butter
2 tablespoons all-purpose flour
1/2 pint whipping cream
   (or half-and-half)
2 tablespoons sherry
1/2 teaspoon salt and pepper
1/2 cup grated cheddar cheese

Slowly thicken butter, flour and cream. Add sherry, salt and pepper. Add crab meat and mix. Sprinkle with the cheddar cheese. Spoon mixture into 4 ramekins and bake at 350 degrees until bubbly, about 15 minutes.

—Mrs. David Wyeth Royster, Jr.
(Annabelle Zeigler Matthews)

Delicious Vegetable Spread

Must prepare 1 day ahead

"The Antique Fair was a fundraiser that brought us, as a League, closer together. We cooked, served and worked very hard, but it was very rewarding. This was something we served that people really enjoyed."

1 envelope unflavored gelatin
1/4 cup cold water
1/4 cup boiling water
2 tomatoes, finely chopped
1 cucumber, finely chopped
1 cup finely chopped celery
1 small green bell pepper, finely chopped
1 small onion, finely chopped
1 pint real mayonnaise

Soak gelatin in 1/4 cup cold water until it begins to soften, then mix in 1/4 cup boiling water and allow to cool. Chop tomatoes and cucumbers and allow to drain thoroughly. Combine all ingredients, including mayonnaise and gelatin, and mix thoroughly. Refrigerate over night and use on crackers or make tea sandwiches, it will make enough for 1 loaf of bread.

—Mrs. Glendall L. King
(Ann Scott "Scotty" Dickinson)
President 1968–1969

Bleu Cheese Biscuits

"To get donations for our Bargain Box, we would host a "Bundles Coffee" for our sustainers. Russian tea, blue cheese biscuits and cucumber sandwiches were enjoyed by all."

1/2 cup crumbled bleu cheese
1/4 butter, softened
1/2 cup all-purpose flour
3/4 cup pecans, chopped

Mix cheese, butter, flour and 1/2 cup chopped pecans. Make into balls. Put 1/4 cup of pecans in blender, blend until finely chopped. Roll the balls in the pecans. Bake at 350 degrees for 15 minutes.

—Mrs. Glendall L. King
(Ann Scott "Scotty" Dickinson)
President 1968–1969

Holiday Pork Roast with Orange Marsala Sauce

Freezes well
Must prepare 1 day ahead
Serves 8

3 pounds pork tenderloin
2/3 cup bottled teriyaki marinade, divided
1 tablespoon plus 1/3 cup dry Marsala wine, divided
3/4 teaspoon finely grated orange peel
2/3 cup orange juice
2 tablespoons cornstarch
4 teaspoons sugar
1/2 cup dried cranberries

Place the pork tenderloin in an extra large ziplock bag. Combine 1/3 cup teriyaki marinade and 1 tablespoon Marsala wine, pour over pork. Turn bag over several times to coat pork well. Refrigerate 8 hours or overnight, turning bag several times. Place pork in shallow roasting pan. Bake at 350 degrees for one hour and 15 minutes, or until thoroughly cooked. Let roast stand 10 minutes before slicing. Meanwhile, combine remaining 1/3 teriyaki marinade, 1/3 cup Marsala wine, orange juice, cornstarch, sugar and 1/2 cup water in medium sauce pan. Bring to boil and simmer until sauce thickens, stir in cranberries and orange peel. Cut pork into slices and serve with sauce.

—Mrs. L.L. Anthony, Jr.
(Nan Sylvester)
President 1970–1971

Martha Washington Creams

May prepare ahead
Makes approximately 2 dozen

"Give these homemade candies with joy! This was my Mother's recipe and has been one of my family's favorite holiday treats!"

1 stick melted margarine
1 box sifted confectioners' sugar
6 squares semi-sweet chocolate (melted)
1 teaspoon vanilla extract
1/4 teaspoon salt
1 inch square paraffin

Stir together melted margarine, sugar, vanilla and salt. Roll into small balls (they will be firm). Melt chocolate and paraffin together in double boiler. Place toothpick in the small balls and dip into the hot chocolate until completely covered. Place on sheet of wax paper to cool. Refrigerate until ready to serve.

—Mrs. Larry K. Petty
(Jane Wornom)
President 1971–1972

Apricot Squares

Freezes well
Makes 16 squares

1/2 pound dried apricots
3/4 cup sugar
3/4 cup water
1 stick real butter
1 cup brown sugar, packed
1 1/4 cups oatmeal
1 1/4 cups all-purpose flour
1 teaspoon baking soda

Grind apricots and mix with the sugar and water. Bring to a boil and cook until thick. Cool. Melt the butter and mix with the brown sugar, oatmeal, flour and soda (add soda to flour before combining with other ingredients). Remove 1 cup of the crumbs. Spread remaining crumbs in a greased 9-square pan. Cover with the apricot mixture, then top with the reserved cup of crumbs. Bake at 350 degrees for 30 minutes.

—Mrs. Ralph Robinson, Jr.
(Sally McConnell)
President 1972–1973

Chocolate Fudge Birthday Cake

"This recipe was passed down to me by my mother, Mary Craig, and made by her for me and my brother and sister at our birthdays every year. I continued this tradition with my own children. The cake has traveled to various cities around the country for birthdays. My children plan to continue this tradition within their own families."

4 (1-ounce) squares unsweetened
   chocolate
1/2 cup sugar
1/2 cup milk
1/2 cup all-vegetable shortening, Crisco
   works best
1 cup sugar
2 eggs
2 cups all-purpose flour, unsifted
1 teaspoon salt
1 cup milk
2 teaspoons vanilla extract
1 teaspoon baking soda dissolved in
   3 tablespoons hot water

Melt chocolate squares with 1/2 cup sugar and 1/2 cup milk and allow to cool. In separate bowl, cream shortening and sugar. Add eggs one at a time. Mix salt with flour and add alternately with milk to batter. Add vanilla and cooled chocolate mixture to batter and mix well. Add soda dissolved in water last and beat until thoroughly mixed. Pour batter into 2 greased and floured 1³/4x9-inch cake pans. Bake at 350 degrees for 30 minutes. Do not overbake but make sure center of cake is done. Let cool in pan for approximately 10 to 15 minutes before removing from cake pans. Let cool completely and ice with Seven-Minute White Icing (recipe to follow).

Seven-Minute White Icing:
2 unbeaten egg whites
1¹/2 cups sugar
5 tablespoons cold water
1/4 teaspoon cream of tartar or,
   1¹/2 teaspoon light corn syrup
1 teaspoon vanilla extract

Place all of the ingredients, except 1 teaspoon vanilla, in the top of a double-boiler and beat until thoroughly blended. Place these ingredients over rapidly boiling water and beat constantly for 7 minutes. Remove the icing from the heat and add 1 teaspoon vanilla. Continue beating until the icing is of spreading consistency. This will ice a two-layer cake.

—Mrs. Hugh F. Bryant
(Mary Lewis Craig)
President 1973–1974

If you are one egg short for a recipe, substitute one teaspoon of cornstarch.

Shrimp and Feta Cheese Vermicelli

May prepare 1 day ahead
Serves 3

4 tablespoons olive oil, divided
1 pound medium shrimp, peeled
pinch of crushed red pepper flakes
2/3 cup crumbled feta cheese
1/2 teaspoon crushed garlic
1 (14.5-ounce) can diced tomatoes
3/4 teaspoon basil
1/2 teaspoon oregano
1/4 teaspoon salt
1/4 teaspoon pepper
1/4 cup dry white wine
8 ounces uncooked vermicelli

Sauté shrimp and red pepper flakes in 2 tablespoons olive oil in large skillet 1 to 2 minutes or until shrimp are slightly pink. Arrange shrimp in a 6x10-inch baking dish. Sprinkle with feta and set aside. Add remaining olive oil to skillet and sauté garlic over low heat. Add tomatoes with juice and cook 1 minute. Stir in wine, basil, oregano, salt and pepper. Simmer, uncovered, 10 minutes. Spoon tomato mixture on shrimp. Bake uncovered at 400 degrees for 10 minutes. Serve over cooked vermicelli.

"I can remember when Consommé Rice was everyone's favorite dish to bring to League covered dish suppers and parties. Of course that was the same time most of our members were wearing "Bee-Hive" hairdos; times certainly have changed."

—Mrs. William A. Current
(Elizabeth Oden)
President 1974–1975

When cooking cabbage, place a small tin cup or can half full of vinegar on the stove near the cabbage. This will absorb the odor from it.

Quick and Easy Broiled Salmon with Herbed Butter

Serve immediately
Serves 8

8 (4- to 6-ounce) salmon steaks
1/4 cup butter or margarine melted
2 tablespoons fresh lemon juice
2 tablespoons chopped parsley
1/4 teaspoon dill weed
1/4 teaspoon salt
1/8 teaspoon coarsely ground pepper

Line broiler pan with heavy duty foil and place salmon on foil. Combine remaining ingredients; baste steaks with mixture. Broil 4 inches from heat, allowing 10 minutes per inch of thickness or until fish flakes easily. Do not turn. Baste several times during cooking. Clean up is a breeze!

"During my term, we made application to the Association of Junior Leagues to become affiliated. A "term paper" type document was prepared, submitted, and the first of three visits came during that year. We were on our way to becoming the Junior League of Gaston County, N.C., Inc."   —Mrs. Tom D. Efird
(Anne Wrightson)
President 1976–1977

Scallops with Mushrooms in Shells

Serve immediately
Serves 6

1/2 cup butter, at room temperature
1 cup thinly sliced mushrooms
3 tablespoons finely chopped shallots
1 tablespoon finely chopped garlic
1 pound fresh bay scallops
1/2 cup soft bread crumbs
1/2 cup finely chopped parsley
salt and pepper

Preheat oven to 450 degrees. Melt 1/4 cup of the butter in a small skillet and add the mushrooms. Cook, stirring often, until the mushrooms are wilted and give up their liquid. Add the shallots and garlic and cook briefly. Spoon the mushroom mixture into a mixing bowl. Cool briefly, then add 2 tablespoons of the remaining butter, the scallops, bread crumbs. Parsley, salt and pepper to taste. Blend well. Use the mixture to fill 6 seafood shells. Arrange the filled shells on a cookie sheet. Melt the rest of the butter and pour it over the mixture in the shells. Bake 10 minutes. If desired, place under broiler until nicely browned, about 1 minute.
—Mrs. David H. Simpson
(Emily Gary)
President 1977–1978

Santa Fe Soup

May prepare ahead
Freezes well
Serves 10

2 pounds lean ground beef

1 large onion, chopped

*2 (1.0-ounce) packages ranch style
dressing mix*

*2 (1.5-ounce) packages Taco seasonings
mix*

*1 (16-ounce) can black beans,
undrained*

*1 (16-ounce) can kidney beans,
undrained*

*1 (16-ounce) can pinto beans,
undrained*

*1 (16-ounce) can diced tomatoes with
chilies, undrained*

*1 (16-ounce) can tomato wedges,
undrained*

*2 (16-ounce) cans white corn,
undrained*

2 cups water

Cook meat and onion together until meat is browned. Stir Ranch style dressing mix and taco seasoning into meat. Add remaining ingredients with juices from all. Simmer for 2 hours, if mixture becomes too thick, add additional water. Garnish each serving with sour cream, shredded cheddar cheese and sliced green onions, if desired. Serve with tortilla chips.

"I thoroughly enjoyed the Follies that the League put on the year I was President. Everyone came together and had a lot of fun, not to mention a lot of money was made and donated to the community."
—Mrs. J. Caswell Taylor, Jr.
(Martha Gullick)
President 1978–1979

Tomato Aspic and Cream Cheese Salad

Serves 12

"When we were applying for membership into the Junior League, we hosted several luncheons for visiting committee members. At one luncheon everyone had to make a tomato aspic, one to test and one to serve. We found ourselves very tired of tomato aspic! However, this is a delicious recipe, especially to serve at a brunch."

8 ounces cream cheese, softened
1/2 cup mayonnaise
1/2 teaspoon salt
2 envelopes unflavored gelatin
1 1/3 tablespoons lemon juice
1/4 cup boiling water
1/2 cup celery, finely chopped
2 tablespoons onions, finely chopped
1/4 cup cold water
1 cup boiling water
1 (16-ounce) can seasoned tomato sauce
2 tablespoons lemon juice
1 teaspoon salt
1/2 bottle capers, drained (optional)

Cheese Layer: Blend softened cream cheese with mayonnaise and salt. Soften 1 teaspoon of the gelatin in lemon juice and dissolve in boiling water. Combine with remaining ingredients and put in bottom of oiled individual molds or one large mold. Chill until firm before adding aspic layer.

Aspic Layer: Soften remaining gelatin in cold water; dissolve in boiling water. Add remaining ingredients and pour over cream cheese layer. (May add 1/2 bottle drained capers for a variation.) Chill until firm.

—Mrs. William J. McLean
(Eva Ann Orr)
President 1979–1980

To remove onion smell from your hands, rub a metal or chrome faucet.

Easy Roasted Chicken

Serve immediately
Serves 4–5

"With a summer spent renovating our newly purchased Bargain Box Building and our Spring Follies production, League members had a very busy year with little time left for the kitchen. Never the less, our resourceful members managed to keep their families well fed with lots of casseroles and one dish meals, just like this one."

1 large fryer
fresh herbs (thyme and rosemary
*   are good)*
1 lemon
1 medium onion, cut into chunks
1 cup white wine
1 cup chicken broth
garlic, salt and pepper to taste
new potatoes
whole baby carrots

Preheat oven to 425 degrees. Squeeze lemon juice into cavity of the chicken. Salt, pepper and garlic the outside. Place chicken in roasting pan. Add onion chunks, fresh herbs, wine and broth. Cover and cook for 45 minutes. Add new potatoes and carrots and continue to cook another 45 minutes.

—Mrs. Joseph Sloan Stowe
(Janice Williamson)
President 1980–1981

1-2-3 Hot Fudge Sauce

Makes approximately 2 cups

"With all of the time and energy it takes to be a Junior League volunteer, this is super easy and a great energy booster!"

1 cup evaporated milk
2 cups sugar
3 squares unsweetened chocolate

Mix together on top of stove and bring to a boil. Remove from heat. Beat 30 seconds with electric mixer. Pour on heaping bowl of ice cream. Leftovers can be kept in the refrigerator and reheated (and beaten again) or eaten straight from the container by the heaping spoonfuls!

—Mrs. Richard L. Voorhees
(Barbara Humphries)
President 1982–1983

Shepherd's Pie
Girl Scout's Shepherd's Pie

Serve immediately
Serves 4

"This is a Girl Scout campfire favorite Ginny Hall and I would make during our camping trips."

1 1/2 pounds ground beef
1 small Vidalia onion
instant mashed potatoes, follow
*   directions based on a serving for 6*
1 cup cheddar cheese, grated
Worcestershire sauce to taste

Brown ground beef. Dice the onion and add to ground beef. Continue to brown. Drain off fat. Add Worcestershire sauce to taste. Set aside. Make mashed potatoes according to directions. Put cooked ground beef and onions in bottom of a loaf size casserole dish. Layer potatoes and grated cheese on top. Put in warm oven until cheese melts.

—Mrs. F.L. Smyre, III
(Priscilla "Brownie" Allen)
President 1983–1984

Serious Tacos with Pintos and Cheese

Serve immediately
Serves 4 –6

"This is our favorite family recipe. Everyone takes part and chops, drains, fills or fries the tacos. At the end of the meal we count the toothpicks on our plates to see who ate the most. We have a friend who holds the record, having eaten 24 tacos in one sitting!"

20 ounce container cooking oil
30 corn tortillas
2 to 3 pounds rump or chuck roast, cooked well and sliced into narrow strips (fajita style)
32 slices American cheese, cut into 1/2 inch strips

Condiments:
1 head lettuce, thinly shredded
2 (14.5-ounce) cans chopped tomatoes, drained
1 small white onion, shredded
jalepeños, chopped (optional)
2 (15.5-ounce) cans pinto beans
12 ounces cheddar cheese, shredded

In deep frying pan or large electric skillet, soften tortillas in 1/2 inch warm oil. Once softened, drain tortillas on newspaper covered with lots of paper towels. As the tortillas are softened and drained, take each tortilla and place strips of roast and American cheese into the center, bring ends together and close tightly with a toothpick. Once all the tortillas are stuffed and fastened, fry them in the same pan. You may need to add oil to return to 1/2 inch, until crispy on both sides. Remove from oil with tongs and drain on paper towels. When preparing to eat, remove toothpick and fill with prepared condiments—lettuce, tomatoes, onions and jalepeños. To prepare the pintos, just heat the beans and add the cheese, allowing the cheese to melt into the beans. Serve along side the tacos.

—Mrs. David R. Stultz
(Jennifer "Jennie" Thomas)
President 1984–1985

Peanut Butter Kisses

Yields approximately 40–45 cookies

"This is David, my son's, favorite cookie. When he was a youngster, his "job" was to unwrap the Kisses. We always had a few extra candies to eat—extra energy for the bakers!"

1 3/4 cups all-purpose flour
1 teaspoon baking soda
1/2 teaspoon salt
1/2 cup shortening
1/2 cup peanut butter
1/2 cup sugar
1/2 cup dark brown sugar, packed
1 egg
2 tablespoons milk
1 teaspoon vanilla extract
1/3 cup additional sugar to roll
  cookie dough
approximately 48 chocolate Kiss candies

Sift together flour, baking soda and salt. Cream shortening, peanut butter, sugar and brown sugar. Add 1 egg blended with milk and vanilla then blend in dry ingredients. Shape rounded tablespoon of dough into ball. Roll lightly in additional sugar. Place on ungreased cookie sheet 2 inches apart. Bake at 375 degrees for 8 minutes. Remove from oven and place chocolate Kiss on top. Lightly twist down into cookie. Return to oven for 2 to 5 minutes. Cool on wire rack.

—Ms. Kathleen Boyle Wofford

Classic Charleston Shrimp Boil

Serve immediately
Serves 6

2 to 3 pounds unshelled medium shrimp
16 new potatoes
4 ears of corn, shucked, broken in half
4 carrots, cut in large chunks
1 pound spicy smoked sausage, such as
  kielbasa, sliced in chunks
1 gallon water
2 1/2 tablespoons Old Bay seasoning

In a 2 to 4 gallon stockpot, bring the water and Old Bay seasoning to a rolling boil. Add the potatoes and sausage chunks; boil 10 minutes. Add the corn and carrots and boil for seven minutes more. Now add the shrimp and boil until the shells turn pink, about 3 to 5 minutes. Drain through a colander and serve with melted butter, cocktail sauce and lots of napkins!

"The 1987–88 Junior League year was the year of the Holiday Home Tour, the publication of the *Southern Elegance* cookbook, NC SPAC meeting, and the NC Art Museum's "Robes of Elegance the Japanese Kimono 16th to 20th Centuries" program—all enduring examples of the influence of many, many volunteer hands at work for their communities."

—Mrs. Theron Dale Ward
(Ann Carroll)
President 1987–1988

Debbie's Pimento Cheese Spread

"My mom is a great cook and I grew up watching her add "a little of this and a little of that"! I've used this recipe as a staple for many covered dishes and as small gifts. Even people who normally don't like pimento cheese eat it!"

24 ounces Cracker Barrel extra sharp cheddar cheese
8 ounce jar diced red pimentos
mayonnaise (the real thing, not low fat)
cider vinegar
1/2 teaspoon sugar
black pepper

Grate the cheese, add the pimentos, undrained. Add a slight capful of cider vinegar, 1/2 teaspoon sugar and a few vigorous shakes of black pepper. Mix all together with the mayonnaise, adding it by large spoonfuls until you reach desired consistency (it usually takes about half of a 32 ounce jar). For a variation: use jalapeños instead of pimentos, or use fresh bell pepper instead of pimentos.

"There are many wonderful experiences I had during my Junior League career, but probably the best was how I matured and grew as a woman by making friends all over the country while traveling as President and President Elect, not to mention how I learned to speak in front of groups!"

—Mrs. Richard C. Brake, Jr.
President 1985–1986
(Deborah Brake)
President 1986–1987

Pasta with Chicken and Creamy Tomato Sauce

Serve immediately
Serves 4

2 tablespoons olive oil
1 pound boneless chicken breasts, cut into 1/2 inch strips
1 large carrot, grated
1 large onion, diced
1 garlic clove, minced
1 (28-ounce) can crushed tomatoes
1 teaspoon salt
1 teaspoon pepper
1/2 cup whipping cream
12 ounces ziti or penne pasta, cooked

Heat oil in skillet over high heat. Add next four ingredients; sauté for 3 minutes, or until meat is thoroughly cooked. Add tomatoes, salt and pepper. Bring to a boil. Reduce heat to low, cover and simmer 10 minutes. Stir in cream and heat thoroughly. Serve over pasta. Freeze any leftover sauce.

—Mrs. Les Davis
(Ann Richardson)
President 1988–1989

Amaretto Custard with Raspberries

May prepare ahead
Serves 6

6 eggs slightly beaten
1/2 cup sugar
2 cups whole milk, scalded
2 tablespoons Amaretto
sweetened whipped cream
2 cups fresh raspberries

Combine eggs and sugar, beating well; gradually add milk, stirring constantly. Stir in Amaretto. Pour into 6 lightly greased, 6 ounce custard cups. Place filled custard cups in 9x13-inch baking pan; pour hot water into pan to a depth of 1 inch. Bake at 375 degrees for 15 to 20 minutes or until knife inserted in custard comes out clean. Remove cups from water and cool. Chill custard thoroughly. Run knife blade around edge of custard cups and unmold on dessert plates. Top with whipped cream, then sprinkle with raspberries.

"The first League meeting I was to preside over was cancelled due to the unexpected arrival of Hurricane Hugo. Our entire city was affected by this devastating storm. We lost 86 trees ourselves and quickly realized the importance of neighbor helping neighbor. Being on the receiving end gave our League a renewed sense of how important it is to help others!"
—Mrs. John Douglas Bridgeman
(Nan Falls)
President 1989–1990

Peanut Butter Pie

Must prepare ahead
Serves 6–8

1 (3-ounce) package cream cheese,
*   softened*
1 cup confectioners' sugar
1/3 cup peanut butter
1/4 cup milk
1 (4-ounce) container whipped topping
1 graham cracker pie crust
1/4 cup finely chopped peanuts or graham
*   cracker crumbs*

Blend cream cheese and confectioners' sugar thoroughly. Beat in peanut butter. Add milk and mix well. Fold in whipped topping by hand and spoon into crust. Top with peanuts or graham cracker crumbs. Chill several hours until firm.

"My year as president saw the League take a step for big grant money for the first time. We were excited to be a part of FACE—Families and Children for Education. We contributed money and volunteers to Woodhill Elementary to help in the classrooms and act as mentors for the parents going through parent training classes and working on their GEDs. The highlight of the year was then Secretary of Education, Lamar Alexander coming to Woodhill to honor the FACE program. It was such a meaningful experience that some of us continued to volunteer long after our placements were over."

—Mrs. Robert S. Pearson
(Jane Baker)
President 1990–1991

Junior League Green Punch

Yields: 15 (6-ounce) servings

"This punch was served at more meetings and parties than I can remember. It was a favorite of all the members!"

24 ounces Sprite or 7-Up
1 (6 ounces) frozen limeade
1 (12 ounces) frozen lemonade
24 ounces water
18 to 24 ounces Rum or Vodka
green food color

Combine all ingredients except the soft drink. Freeze for 48 hours. Remove one hour before serving, mash down in bowl and add the 24 ounces of soft drink.

—Mrs. Roy E. Lockett
(Donna Colvin)
President 1991–1992

Ice Cream Sandwiches

Freezes well
Makes 6 bars

1/2 cup light corn syrup
1/2 cup chunky peanut butter
4 cups Rice Krispies
1 pint vanilla ice cream, softened

Combine corn syrup and peanut butter, mixing well. Add rice cereal. Stir until cereal is well coated. Press into a 9x13-inch pan and freeze until firm. Cut into a dozen 3-inch bars. Slice or spoon ice cream onto 6 of the bars and top with the other 6 to make ice cream sandwiches. Wrap sandwiches individually in Saran Wrap—they won't last long enough to get freezer burn!

Note: This recipe can be altered to personal preference by using different flavors of frozen dessert.

—Mrs. Timothy A. Grooms
(Candy Rapier)
President 1992–1993

Baking powder will remove tea or coffee stains from china pots or cups.

Southwestern Hashbrown Casserole

May prepare ahead
Serves 6

2¹/2 cups frozen hash brown potatoes
¹/2 cup chopped broccoli
¹/2 cup mild salsa
2 tablespoons chopped onion
salt and pepper
6 beaten eggs (or enough to cover
     casserole)
milk
1 cup each of grated cheddar cheese and
     mozzarella cheese

Preheat oven to 350 degrees. Sauté hashbrowns in skillet. Spray 9x13-inch pan with vegetable spray. Layer potatoes, broccoli, salsa, onions, salt and pepper. Beat eggs with a small amount of milk. Pour just enough to cover the layered ingredients in the pan. (May refrigerate overnight at this point, bring to room temperature before baking) Cook for 30 minutes or until eggs are done. Remove from oven and add grated cheeses and return to oven long enough for cheese to melt. Cut into squares and serve hot.

—Mrs. David Russell Kirlin
(Nancy "Nan" DeChristofor)
President 1993–1994

Trash Mix

This recipe seems appropriate since Jennie served as president twice, we liked her so much we decided to "recycle" her!

May prepare ahead.
Serves 10

1 stick butter
1 cup crunchy peanut butter
1 package butterscotch morsels
1 box Crispix cereal
powdered sugar

Melt butter and peanut butter in a medium spaucepan over low heat. Mixture will be lumpy. Remove from heat. Stir in morsels until melted. In a large mixing bowl combine cereal with melted mixture. Stir cereal until completely coated. Spread mix on a cookie sheet and allow to dry, almost completely—about 30 minutes. Put powdered sugar in a bag and place mix in bag. Shake well.

My second term as League president was like cooking with an old familiar recipe. Some "ingredients" were new, like a great group of new actives, and this added spice. Some were familiar which added ease to the recipe. This made for an exciting mix and a great year!

—Mrs. David R. Stultz
(Jennifer "Jennie" Thomas)
President 1994–1995

Shogun Salmon

Serves 4

1/2 cup sherry, Marsala or port
2 tablespoons fresh parsley, chopped
2 teaspoons sugar or honey
2 tablespoons prepared horseradish
1/4 cup soy sauce
1/2 teaspoon black pepper
*1 1/2 pounds Alaskan Salmon steaks or
    fillets*
5 green onions, chopped
2 tablespoons vegetable or sesame oil

Mix first six ingredients. Place salmon in shallow flat dish and pour marinade over fish. Sprinkle green onions over the top. Cover and refrigerate for 1/2 hour. Turn and refrigerate 1/2 hour more. Spray grill with cooking spray. Place fish on grill. Add the 2 tablespoons of oil to reserved fish marinade and keep fish moist with marinade. Grill 7 minutes on first side, turn and repeat for 5 minutes or until fish flakes easily with a fork. It is very important not to over cook, or the salmon will be dry.

—Mrs. Mark N. Couture
(Annemarie Nelson)
President 1995–1996

To help stuffed peppers keep their shape while baking, put them in muffin tins or individual baking cups.

Shortbread Cookies

"It was a thrill and honor to be able to present a check for $40,000 to Barbara Bush at a Gaston Literacy Council meeting. Following the meeting was a reception where shortbread cookies were served and they were a big hit!"

1³/4 cups all-purpose flour
3 tablespoons sugar
1/2 cup butter (not margarine)

Combine flour and sugar. Cut in butter until mixture resembles fine crumbs and starts to cling. Knead the dough until smooth. Turn dough onto floured surface and pat or roll dough to 1/2-inch thickness. Cut into strips or use a cookie cutter and place cookies on ungreased cookie sheet and bake at 325 degrees for 20 minutes, or until bottoms begin to slightly brown (do not overcook).

—Miss Cheryl Black
President 1996–1997

Terri's Chicken Pot Pie

Serves 4

4 chicken breasts cooked, deboned and
cubed or shredded
1/2 teaspoon thyme
2 (10³/4-ounce) cans cream of
chicken soup
2 cups chicken broth
1 (15-ounce) can mixed vegetables
1¹/2 tablespoons vermouth
2 pie shells, uncooked

Mix first six ingredients together. Pour chicken mixture into pie shells and bake at 400 degrees until browned.

—Mrs. Phillip W. Nixon
(Terri Buting)
President 1997–1998

When rolling cookie dough, sprinkle board with confectioners' sugar instead of flour. Too much flour makes the dough heavy.

Index

Southern Elegance A SECOND COURSE

Junior League of Gaston County, N. C.
2950 South Union Road, Suite A
Gastonia, North Carolina 28054
704.853.8502

Your Order	Qty	Total
Southern Elegance A Collection of the Best of Carolina Cuisine $15.95 ea. _____		$_____
Southern Elegance A Second Course $17.95 ea. _____		$_____
North Carolina residents add 6% sales tax . . . . _____		$_____
Postage and handling $3.50 ea. . . . . _____		$_____
Total		$_____

_____
Name

_____
Street Address

_____
City   State   Zip

_____
Telephone

Method of Payment: [   ] VISA   [   ] MasterCard
                    [   ] Check enclosed payable to *Southern Elegance* A Second Course

_____
Account Number   Expiration Date

_____
Signature

Photocopies accepted.